PRIESTS AND PHILOSOPHERS.

BY THE

REV. W. GRESLEY,

VICAR OF BOYNE HILL, AND PREBENDARY OF LICHFIELD.

LONDON:

JOSEPH MASTERS, 78, NEW BOND STREET.

MDCCCLXXIII.

LONDON:
PRINTED BY J. MASTERS AND SON,
ALBION BUILDINGS, BARTHOLOMEW CLOSE, E.C.

PREFACE.

I HAVE endeavoured in the following pages to set forth the relative position of GOD's Ministers, and those philosophers of the present day who oppose their ministrations. I have carefully endeavoured to avoid the prevailing error of complimenting men for their cleverness whose principles I utterly condemn. My aim has been to speak strongly and in plain terms of the fearful wrong which non-Christian philosophers are doing; nor have I scrupled to laugh at their absurdities.

Surely in these days of light and knowledge to mistake in the great object for which life is given us is the height of folly, and to lead others into the same state of error is to be the instrument of the greatest wrong which can be committed.

I heartily wish that others more able than myself would speak out what they must surely feel.

CONTENTS.

PRIESTS AND PHILOSOPHERS.

CHAPTER I.

IT is an unfortunate circumstance of the present
times that the Ministers of CHRIST are obliged to
defend themselves and their flocks against the
attacks of men who ought in truth to be amongst
the greatest helps in forwarding the glory of
GOD, but who most strangely have come to be
amongst the principal adversaries of religious
truth,—I mean, of course, some who call themselves Philosophers and men of science.

Half a century ago science was confined chiefly
to the few who specially devoted themselves to its
cultivation, and was but little canvassed by the
public. Now, on the contrary, scientific men
court popularity and influence. They have their

B

public meetings, and get together a number of
ladies and gentlemen to hear and admire them.
They have their magazines and reviews in which
scientific subjects are discussed. In short, they
seem to wish the different branches of science to
be brought as much as possible before the public.
And what is much to be noted, the public meetings on science, and the discussions in periodicals,
at least in some of them, are not directed to the
enlargement of science by new discoveries,—new
discoveries are made in the study or the labora-
tory by the devoted workers in each department;
but all this public discussion seems to have rather
an ethical bearing. It answers the purpose of
Church Congresses, Nonconformist gatherings,
Conservative and Radical meetings, and its design
is to influence the minds of men with regard to
the moral value of science in comparison with
other departments of knowledge. Scientific men
aspire to exercise a control over the belief and
conduct of the present generation. I am myself
no enemy of science,—far from it: I used to take
much interest in it before my time and thoughts
were occupied by the duties of the priesthood.
I greatly admire the ability of those who have so
much enlarged the boundaries of science in the
last and present generation. And, I believe, that
rightly viewed, science is calculated to advance
the highest interests of mankind. And this is

in truth the line of argument which I propose to take—namely, to point out the true value of science and its bearing on the moral and intellectual advancement of the human race.

I wish to treat the subject in a popular manner, and, if I should sometimes seem to speak rather lightly of what men of science deem important matters, and which really are so, if rightly viewed, I hope they will believe that I have no sort of prejudice against science itself, but only a doubt, or rather a conviction, that the subject has not always been treated in the most rational and advantageous manner.

An amusing paper appeared in the April number of *Macmillan's Magazine*, in which "that able and eminent man of science, Mr. Wallace," as the editor calls him, "puts forth in strong and uncompromising terms a plan for the practical and beneficial mode of applying the national property now held by the Church, and of preserving and utilizing for national objects the parish churches and other ecclesiastical buildings spread so thickly over our land, and which constitute a picturesque and impressive record of much of our social and religious history for more than a thousand years."

Mr. Wallace's plan is simply this,—to abolish all rectors, vicars, and incumbents of the Church of England; at least, to relieve them all of their property; or rather to suffer the present occupants to die out without appointing others; and substitute in their places certain national parochial rectors, who need be of no particular religion, "but shall be up to the highest intellectual level of the age," and shall before their appointment "pass a much more rigid examination, and furnish better evidence of temper and moral character (!) than is now required,—men of intellectual culture, refined manners, and moral character," "and above all things, free from sectarian teaching." "The narrow education, imperfect training, and sectarian prejudices of the clergy of the Established Church (!) prevent their opinions having much weight, either with the public at large or the Government. But the national rector would be in a very different position."

There is one great objection, Mr. Wallace thinks, to this plan of abolishing the Church of England, and substituting these secular rectors. Some people may think it Utopian! To destroy the Church of GOD root and branch, confiscate the endowments which have been given by the piety of our ancestors, in order that the poor as well as the rich throughout the land might be instructed in their duty to GOD and man, to deprive hundreds, thousands perhaps, of our parishes of Christian instruction and sacraments, of a minister of religion, who shall baptize their children, marry their young men and maidens, bury their dead,—to hand over their parsonages and glebes to secular men, and make our ancient churches places "for interesting and instructive series of lectures,"—the chief objection to this notable scheme is that it may be thought Utopian! too good to be practicable! Well, that is an odd way of putting it. At any rate, it shows what philosophers have got in their heads. Mr. Wallace's scheme, if brought about, would have the advantage of securing some 5,000 or 6,000 nice appointments for his brother philosophers, who, he says, shall be "as good as judges."

It would be a curious thing to speculate what could be the object of a man like Mr. Wallace in writing such an article. The editor himself thinks it right to apologise for its insertion. "The views," he says, "set forth in the following article may strike many of the readers of *Macmillan* as both novel and hazardous, ... inadequate, or even problematical." The chief value of them is to show the animus of a particular party, the intense scorn and dislike with which they regard the ministers of God's Church, the way in which they would treat them if they got the chance. Mr. Wallace's conclusion is worth considering as showing the notions of his party. "We are," he says, "actually in the possession of an elaborate organization, and an ample property handed down to us by our forefathers, with whom it did at one time fulfil many of the high functions which I wish to restore to it. We have suffered it to remain in the hands of *a narrow religious corporation,* which in no sufficient degree represents either the most cultivated intelligence, or the highest morality of the age, and which by its dogmatic theology and resistance to progress, has become out of harmony both with the best and least educated portion of the community." How sad it is that a man like Mr. Wallace should thus vilify and insult a body of men like the English clergy. I do not think that the clergy have any such bitter, ill-natured feeling against men of science, as Mr. Wallace exhibits against the clergy. When the Christian religion is attacked, it is, of course, their bounden duty to stand up for what they conscientiously believe to be truth. They would be cowards and traitors if they did not. Why should philosophers adopt this tone towards them? Mr. Wallace is, I believe, a fair specimen of his class. Surely he cannot be so ignorant of the state of things in this civilized land as to believe that our bishops and clergy generally can be justly charged with sectarian prejudices, narrow education, imperfect training. He must be aware that there are amongst the more eminent of them men of the

highest culture, and the most enlarged views,—
that there is no body of men throughout the
world more devoted to their self-chosen task of
doing all the good they can in their generation.

Another gentleman, a writer in the *Contemporary Review* for September, 1873, asks, " Are not
the clergy notorious for their rancour, their
narrow-mindedness, their multiform prejudices,
their incapacity for seeing truth in any other
aspect than that in which old world formularies
exhibit it ? Have they any sympathy with the
restless activity which marks the age ?" What is
all this but saying that the clergy do not agree
with this writer in his opinions, and think that
religious truth is something fixed and enduring,
not an affair of " restless activity ?" Whence
arises this tone of asperity against men, who, as
a body, are devoted to the spiritual and temporal
good of mankind ? It is a sad and unworthy
jealousy. But the case being so, I see no help
for it, but that the clergy and their friends should
defend themselves with all their strength against
these most uncourteous and unwarrantable attacks,—not in the same spirit of supercilious
contempt, but with the calm and strong sense of
confident rectitude.

Amongst our nineteenth-century philosophers
none is more dogmatic and pugnacious than
Professor Huxley. Most men of science endea-

vour, or at least affect, to reconcile science with
the Christian Faith. Professor Huxley, on the
contrary, does his utmost to show their discrepancy. "The improver of natural knowledge,"
he says, "absolutely refuses to acknowledge
authority as such. For him scepticism is the
highest of duties: blind faith the one unpardonable sin. And it cannot be otherwise, for every
great advance in natural knowledge has involved
the absolute rejection of authority, the cherishing
the keenest scepticism, the annihilation of the
spirit of blind faith. . . . The man of science has
learned to believe in justification, not by faith, but
by verification." ("Lay Sermons," p. 22.) Again,
—"The whole of modern thought is steeped in
science. . . . The greatest intellectual revolution
mankind has ever yet seen is now slowly taking
place by its agency." (P. 130.) "Plague, pestilence, and famine, are admitted by *all but fools*
[those, for instance, who say their prayers in
church] to be the natural result of causes for
the most part fully within human control, and not
the unavoidable tortures inflicted by wrathful
Omnipotence upon His helpless handiwork." (P.
311.) Thank you, Mr. Professor, you are very
polite. Some have thought that the folly is not
all on our side.

" Go, wondrous creature, mount where Science guides,
Go, measure earth, weigh air, and state the tides,

Instruct the planets in what orbs to run,
Correct old Time, and regulate the sun.

    *   *   *   *

Go, teach Eternal Wisdom how to rule,
Then drop into thyself, and be—a fool."—POPE.

What must strike the readers of these extracts
is the curiously unfair and illogical manner in
which the philosopher seems to think that he can
take in the unwary by a dexterous handling of
words. One is almost surprised that a man of
Professor Huxley's knowledge of the world should
for one moment imagine that his readers were so
simple as to be deceived by such verbiage. He
declares that none but fools imagine that plague,
pestilence, and famine are the "unavoidable tortures inflicted by wrathful Omnipotence upon His
helpless handiwork." Evidently this does not
touch this question. What the philosopher has
to prove is no such nonsense as this; but that
plague, pestilence, and famine are not the just
judgments of Almighty GOD upon sinners, which,
nevertheless, may be averted for the most part
by timely repentance.

Take, again, the expression used in the former
extract—" Scepticism," he says, " is the highest
of duties ; *blind* faith the unpardonable sin . . . .
every great advancement in natural knowledge has
involved the absolute rejection of authority, the
cherishing of the keenest scepticism, the annihilation of the spirit of blind faith." *Blind*

faith! Does not the professor see that the very
epithet which he puts in for the sake apparently
of strengthening his argument, absolutely annihi-
lates it? Who ever advocated a blind faith?
One would think he had in his mind the case of
people taken in by some foolish hoax, and was
warning his readers against being made April
fools. It is not a *blind* faith, but a reasonable
faith, an enlightened faith—a holy, loving faith—
that is the sort of faith which the Christian advocates—not a blind faith. Faith, says an excellent
writer, "is the highest act of reason, because it
is a reliance on perfect Wisdom and Truth."
And not only in religion, but in every department of life, it may be safely said, that a reasonable faith, a due regard for testimony, a just
deference to authority, is the basis of the whole
human system. Suppose Professor Huxley, in
his good nature, condescended to explain to an
unsophisticated rustic some of the well-known
facts or principles of science, and told him that
the sun stood stationary in the heavens, and the
earth was a spherical globe continually moving;
he would be rather disgusted if his pupil turned
round upon him, "Don't tell me such a pack of
stuff—don't I see the sun rise every morning in
the east, and move across the sky to the west?
and, surely, I may believe my own eyes. And as
to the earth being round, I once went twenty

miles by rail and it was as flat as a bowling-green
all the way." Would our philosopher applaud
the man's scepticism as the highest of all duties,
and congratulate him on having avoided the
unpardonable sin of blind faith? Or would he
not rather set him down a conceited ass? So,
if a clergyman spoke to one of his parishioners of
the great mercy of GOD in sending the former and
latter rains, and reserving the appointed weeks for
harvest, and exhorted him to be thankful to GOD
for causing the corn to grow in the fields, and
the fruits in their season; it would be rather a
disappointment for him to hear in answer to his
pious exhortation, "Don't tell me about GOD
making the things to grow, I tell you they all
grow of themselves; you have nothing to do but
sow what you want, wheat or potatoes, or man-
gold-wurzel, and they come up of their own
accord. If it's a good season we have a good
crop, and if it's a bad one, why we have a bad
crop, that's all." O most amiable sceptic, most
rare philosopher! the Professor would say.
Others, perhaps, would think the man simply a
fool.

It may be worth while to carry out our illustration of this "highest of duties" somewhat further.
We surely may suppose our sceptical working
man—nay, we may hear him, I fear—going
much beyond this in his scepticism. "You

tell me of a GOD that rules the world, and about
heaven and hell, but I don't believe a word of it.
You tell us if we get drunk, and swear, and steal,
and do other wicked things, we shall go to hell.
I never saw anybody who had been to hell; how
am I to know there is such a place ? It is all very
well for you rich people who have got hold of all
the good things of the world to try and keep us
poor folks contented, by telling us we shall go to
heaven if we are good, and to hell if we are
wicked. But we're not children now, we have
learned to be philosophers, and know a thing or
two. If it was not for the police, and the soldiers,
we would soon help ourselves to some of the
things which you keep so safe now. You gentry
have got some good wine in your cellars, and
plate and money in your houses. Perhaps before
long we shall come and help ourselves, and take
our chance of going to hell for it."

This is simply the carrying out of Professor
Huxley's philosophy, " the cherishing the keenest
scepticism and the annihilation of the spirit of
blind faith."

To my mind the truest philosophy would teach
us that most human affairs rest on faith—not a
blind faith, but a reasonable and enlightened
faith. When the first ideas break on the mind
of a child it is faith in his parents' instruction
which is the medium through which he obtains

knowledge. At school the authority of his teacher is the chief means of his advancement in culture. What are the first lectures of the Professor but authoritative exhibitions of the principles of science? If the pupil refused to accept anything which was not made perfectly plain to his understanding he would make but poor progress in art or science. How can a man possibly learn anything about geography if he disbelieves in the existence of any country which he has not seen? How is it possible to prove to any man that England and Ireland are two separate islands, or that America is on the other side of the Atlantic, or that London has nearly three millions of inhabitants, and that the Lord Mayor lives at the Mansion House, or that the Queen went last week from Windsor to Balmoral, or that the funds rose $\frac{3}{8}$ per cent. yesterday—if people will not believe anything which cannot be proved to demonstration?

Of course there is such a thing as credulity. Men have believed many lies to their cost. Many have been deluded by designing agitators, by sceptical writers, to their eternal ruin. Eve believed the Devil when he told her that she might eat of the forbidden fruit and not die. Sinful curiosity caused her ruin. The Christian preacher declares to men that there is a great God of Heaven and Earth, the Maker and Ruler

of the universe, our Friend and FATHER. He
recounts the history of our LORD JESUS CHRIST,
which has been handed down by infallible testimony, believed by the Church for eighteen hundred years, accepted by the best and wisest of
men, as the rule of life and the hope of immortality. The philosophers (some philosophers, I
should say) tell us there is no GOD Who is the
Maker and Ruler of all things; that the visible
world came he cannot tell how, and goes on of its
own accord, that there is no heaven or hell, no
responsibility after this life. Our moral condition now as for eternity depends on which testimony we will accept. The Christian Divine has
the testimony of ages, the authority of the best
and wisest: the philosopher has nothing to allege
in behalf of his scepticism, but his own private
opinion. But then the system which he upholds
has this advantage—that it allows him who embraces it to follow the devices of his own heart,
indulge freely his lusts and passions without
fear of future retribution; and so, not without
misgivings, he accepts it. The heart of another
is accessible to Divine grace; he acknowledges
the justice and the love of GOD, recognizes the
power and the wisdom of the Great Ruler of
Heaven, and yields himself in humble obedience
to the laws. One believes and is saved; the
other refuses to believe and is lost.

With all his obvious incapacity to judge of the various sources of knowledge, Mr. Huxley is singularly contemptuous of those who differ from him. "If," he says, "man is not to be considered a reasoning being, unless he asks what his sensations are, and why they are, what is a Hottentot, or an Australian black-fellow, or what the 'swinked hedger' of an ordinary agricultural district ?—*nay, what becomes of an average country squire or parson ?*" I know nothing of the Professor's antecedents, his birth, parentage, and education. But I certainly supposed that he had sufficient knowledge of the world and of the usages of society, to be aware that this sort of contemptuous language with regard to classes of persons is not becoming. It is perhaps too much the habit of controversialists to flatter each other with over-smooth language, but this writer goes out of his way to show his contempt. One would think he knew nothing of country squires and parsons but from Fielding's description of Squire Western and Parson Adams in the last century —even then caricatures. He seems quite unaware that men of highest culture are to be found amongst those whom he ridicules, and that as classes the English clergy and landowners of the present generation, might well be compared for manly intelligence with any other classes in the world.

I would venture to propose that a mutual compact should be entered into between Priests and Philosophers, namely, that while contending earnestly for the Truth, they should abstain from calling names and using opprobrious epithets one towards another. Must not Mr. Wallace admit, in his calmer moments, that it is not highly cultured language, when he says of the clergy that they are " a narrow religious corporation which in no sufficient degree represents the most cultivated intelligence or the highest morality of the age," implying that they are both ignorant and immoral? Must not Professor Huxley regret that he has written such language as that " none but fools pray to be delivered from ' plague, pestilence and famine ?' " I, for my part, strongly advise my friends to refrain from calling men of science, even if they be uncourteous and provoking, " philosophical prigs" or " addle-pated professors." It would tend very much to the maintenance of Christian courtesy if such epithets were abstained from on both sides. At the same time I would never counsel the abstinence from plain and serious speaking. A spade should be called a spade. If a man does not believe in GOD I see not by what other name he can be designated but an atheist; if a man rejects the Christian religion he is an infidel; if he believes in a sort of *anima mundi*, or law or order of nature, he is a pantheist. So, if a man believes the doctrines of the Christian Church he should be called orthodox, or bigoted, if you please, for that means earnest and zealous. But we object to be called " Bibliolaters," " Philistines," fanatics, and the like. Surely our differences might be more profitably discussed without the use of such unparliamentary language.

CHAPTER II.

NO SORT OF REASON FOR THIS UNNATURAL JEALOUSY BETWEEN PHILOSOPHERS AND DIVINES.—PHILOSOPHERS MOST IN THE WRONG.—THE QUESTION TESTED BY THE NUMBER OF EMINENT MEN ON EITHER SIDE.

THIS unnatural jealousy between divines and philosophers is the more to be deplored because there is really no cause for it. Each party might pursue its separate course if it would, without collision—nay, rather, with mutual benefit. Unhappily an evil influence has come between them. And I must say that the chief blame rests with the philosophers, though, strangely enough, they seem to think that the theologians are to blame. "In this nineteenth century," says Professor Huxley, "as at the dawn of modern physical science, the cosmogony of the semi-barbarous Hebrew, is the incubus of the philosopher, and the opprobrium of the orthodox. Who can number the patient and earnest seekers after truth, from the days of Galileo until now, whose lives have been embittered, and their good name blasted by the mistaken zeal of bibliolaters? Who can count the host of weaker men whose sense of truth has been destroyed in the effort to harmonize impossibilities, whose life has been wasted in the attempt to force the generous new wine of science into the old bottles of Judaism ?"[1] This is not fair or candid. Surely the Christian minister might say with much more truth and sadness, Who shall number the once Christian souls, once hopeful of salvation through CHRIST, whose minds have been perplexed, whose lives have been embittered, and, alas it is too probable, whose souls have been lost by the thoughtless cavils, and ill-considered theories, and rash speculations of so-called philosophers vaunting the flavour of the new wine of science when the old is better. Who can contemplate without a shudder the eternal consequence to immortal souls of the vagaries of science falsely so called ?

Theologians are not at all disposed to thwart or to disparage men of science in their own department. It is only when philosophers needlessly interfere in matters which do not belong to them, that religious zeal and truthfulness force the divine to resist intrusion into his province. When men of science have made some real discovery, the Christian divine at once acquiesces. A century ago the general opinion was that this earth which we inhabit was about 6,000 years old. When

[1] Lay Sermons, 305. No. 2.

geologists brought forward evidence that its history covered millions of ages, the theologians recognised cheerfully the truth of the discovery. And so they do always gladly hail any of the really great and magnificent discoveries of science. But when the man of science broaches a theory that there was no Creator,—or that the Creator takes no care of the work which He has made, but suffers it to take its course under fixed and immutable laws, the Christian divine rightly demands some proof of his assertions. When another man of science sets himself against the whole course of Christian opinion, and asserts that man, instead of being created by GOD in His own image, is but the development of an ape, or that the ancestors of civilized man were mere savages, that to believe in miracles is impossible, something of a feeling of indignation naturally springs up in the mind of the Christian at hearing such reckless assertions made without the shadow of proof or even probability. I do not think that some of our modern philosophers allow themselves to consider how extremely offensive it is to those who conscientiously believe the Bible, and whose whole lives are directed in conformity with its doctrines,—to hear what they are accustomed to reverence quietly set aside by men who really have no evidence whatever to show for many of their opinions, who deliberately reject

all the accustomed rules of logical argument.
What can possibly fill the mind of a Christian
minister with greater pain and sorrow than when
a philosopher recklessly and cruelly endeavours
to disparage the efficacy of prayer for instance,
which is the very key-stone of holiness here, and
happiness hereafter?

I would just ask the sceptical philosopher to
compare together the results of the two systems.
First, let him ask himself what would be the consequence to mankind if it turned out that Christianity was a fable: secondly, what would be the
consequences if it turned out that his own philosophy, so far as it contradicted Christianity, was
entirely false.   Supposing for a moment that this
world were the only scene of our existence, and
that the Resurrection and Judgment were myths,
how would mankind have been affected as regards
the concerns of this world only, if they were persuaded to live as Christians?   Is it not a fact
that there are twenty thousand clergy in England
alone, spread over the country, whose duty and
occupation it is to do all the good they can to
those amongst whom they live, to train up the
young in habits of truth and honesty, to incul-
cate amongst the people the principles of good
conduct, charity, conscientiousness,—to spread
everywhere the moral teachings of CHRIST and
His Apostles?   " Blessed are the pure in heart,

for they shall see GOD. Blessed are the merciful, for they shall receive mercy. Be kindly affectioned one to another with brotherly love. Abhor that which is evil, cleave to that which is good. Rejoice with them that do rejoice, and weep with them that weep. Recompense no man evil for evil. Provide things honest in the sight of all men. Let us walk honestly as in the day, not in rioting and drunkenness, not in chambering and wantonness, not in strife and envying. Owe no man anything, but to love one another." Will the opponent of Christianity venture to assert that the constant presentation of precepts like these to the minds of the people has not very largely the effect of producing the results of virtue and honest living : that there are multitudes of good men and women who have been influenced to lead just and holy lives by the inculcation of Christian precepts,—not to speak now of the eternal benefits which we who are believers in CHRIST have no doubt will result from a life of faith and virtue.

Take now the contrary view, suppose the infidel philosopher to establish an opinion amongst men generally that Christian doctrine is a fable, will he not subvert to a great extent all these cogent and holy principles, destroy the most effectual motive in men to live righteously and conscientiously ? Then suppose it turns out that

he is mistaken,—suppose the last day reveals to
him that his opposition to religion has been a
false and wicked proceeding, what will be the
horror of the disclosure? He is a man, we will
say, who has written scientific treatises, clever
articles in opposition to the Christian faith, made
some good hits against the clergy. But suppose
him to be wrong,—suppose he has been the
cause of consigning the souls of hundreds of his
fellow-men to eternal ruin,—some perhaps who
were near and dear to him, who looked to him for
instruction and support. What inconceivable
remorse awaits him! Nor is this all, for the influence of a man extends beyond his own generation,—the evil which he has caused will go on
perhaps increasing,—will never die. For endless
ages he will lament the wilfulness, or the vanity,
or the malignity which has made him the instrument of so much evil.

These are terrible thoughts. Surely the possibility of being the instrument of so much evil
must, one would think, have some effect in deter-
ring men from so reckless a course, when it is
certain that in so doing they are setting themselves against the opinion of the wisest and best
men in the civilized world. I would ask the
philosophic infidel, to consider whether the great
mass of intellectual opinion is not ranged against
him. Let him for a moment disembarrass him-

self of the influence of his own particular clique,
and reflect whether the men of highest intellect
are not decidedly opposed to him. Let him advert to the fact that the most eminent men of
the age in which he lives are, beyond question,
believers in Christianity. Without expressing
any opinion on Mr. Gladstone's politics, it is unquestionable that he is a man of the highest
intellect. Mr. Gladstone we know has written
several works advocating the truth and position
of the Christian Church; and has very recently
in a speech publicly declared his adherence to
the Christian faith, and pointedly blamed the
proceedings of those who would subvert it. The
present Lord Chancellor has, I believe, published
a volume of Christian Hymns. The late Lord
Chancellor has for many years of his life taught
the little children in a Sunday School. Lord
Derby, or his father, I forget which, wrote a
book on the LORD's Parables for his God-child.
The late Speaker of the House of Commons
set on foot a Commentary on the Holy Scriptures for the express purpose of counteracting
the influence of infidels. The Duke of Argyll
has written several books on Christian subjects.
Which, amongst men of any eminence, can be
quoted as taking the opposite view, and publicly
assailing Christianity? I cannot call to mind
any one of higher character for intellect and

culture than the Duke of Somerset, and even he does not go nearly so far as some of our philosophic sceptics. I do not of course cite either divines on one side, or philosophers on the other, but merely call on the men of highest intellect in the age to decide between them, and I think that a comparison of eminent Christians, who openly maintain the truth of God's Revelation, with those who oppose it, ought at least to abate something from the tone of confidence with which philosophic infidels are wont to assert their views.

Oh! it is a hazardous game which these men are playing, lightly as they may think or speak. The fate of nations, the salvation or ruin of millions of immortal souls is involved in the question of the truth of Christianity. How men of common humanity or common sense should dare to venture on the tremendous responsibility of endeavouring to subvert the faith of the generation in which they live is an insoluble paradox. One would think that a man tainted with infidelity would shrink from contact with his fellow-men, like one infected with the plague, lest he should inadvertently be the means of conveying to others the fatal epidemic.

CHAPTER III.

IT seems to be assumed by men of science, if
not by others, that science is an unquestionable
and undoubted good to the whole human race;
and that every advance in science is to be hailed
with the greatest satisfaction. Of course, no one
would be so rash as to affirm that it is an evil,
but still I think it may be worth while to try and
estimate its real value, and to ascertain whether
we are making the best use of it. .

We all feel and understand that it is very desirable to know the nature of all the wonderful
things which surround us in the present world,
and the laws by which the universe is governed.
Take, for instance, one of the commonest, at the
same time the most stupendous, of the laws of the
universe—which strangely, as it almost seems, was
not known to men of former generations, but now
forms part of every one's store of knowledge—
namely, that day and night are caused by the

revolution of the earth round its axis, and not, as
would appear to the eye, by the motion of the
sun round the earth. One is almost tempted to
think that the people who lived in the world
under the strange old notion must have been an
inferior race to those of recent generations. Philosophers and popular writers are never tired of
laughing at the stupid old Pope, who shut up
Galileo in the prison of the Inquisition. Some
even speak of the story as being, in some way or
other, a disgrace to religion. But, desirable as it
is to know the truth about the earth turning on
its axis, it is obvious, if we think of it, that the
knowledge has but little influence on the moral
well-being of the human family. There were men
as good, as noble, as wise before Copernicus as
after—wise I mean in the government of states,
or of their families, or of their own spirit. Without for a moment denying the value of even
theoretical science, yet it seems undeniable that
such knowledge, viewed merely as knowledge, is
of comparatively small value as regards man's
moral condition.

It would, of course, be better to find out if we
could, what is the nature and use of comets; to
know more than we do at present about storms,
and drought, and the coming seasons—not that
we could help ourselves much, or regulate them,
if we knew them perfectly; yet it would be a

satisfaction. So it is well to investigate the in-
finitesimal minuteness of the works of creation. It
is a satisfaction to know how many animalcules
there are in a drop of ditch water; what is the
construction of the foot of a fly, which enables it
to walk about on the ceiling—not that we can
ever hope to emulate the feat: still it is curious
and interesting. It is well to know about proto-
plasm, and the germs of animal and vegetable
life, and the peculiar affections of the heart of a
tortoise, or " the regeneration of the eyes of a
crab" (subjects recently discussed before the
scientific societies of London and Paris), or Mr.
Darwin's recent subject, " The Legitimate and
Illegitimate Union between the two kinds of
Primrose." It is well to know the secondary
causes of things, and not merely to say that " GOD
hath made them so," though that, after all, is the
true origin of all things. The scientific investigation of these apparently minute matters may
lead to further medical discoveries, and enable us
to meet the ravages of cholera, diphtheria, &c.

But the advocate of science will of course say,
that whatever may be our estimate of the value
of science theoretically, there can be no doubt of
its immense practical value as regards all the uses
of life. This is admitted; we have in the present age a thousand luxuries and conveniences
unknown to our forefathers—for which we ought

to be duly thankful. Take only, by way of
illustration, the rapidity and convenience of
travelling in the present day—this is due to
science.   Dr. Black discovered the power of
latent heat, and the "immortal Watt" applied
it to locomotion.   Let me suppose Professor
—— addressing the ladies and gentlemen of the
Brighton meeting, and comparing the old-
fashioned mode of travelling with the present.
We will suppose a young lady of distinction
setting out to pay a visit to her friends in the
country about the time when Chaucer wrote his
Canterbury Tales.   She would make her journey
on horseback; perhaps, on a pillion behind a
serving-man.   Then there would be three or four
others to carry the luggage, armed with swords
and bucklers to defend her against highwaymen.
The journey would take three or four days, and
the nights must be spent at old inconvenient
hostelries.   At last, after various perils, she gets
to her friend's house or castle, weary with her
long ride, and oh ! when she comes to unpack her
luggage, only think, of the way in which her best
dresses must be all crushed and crumpled after a
long journey in old-fashioned mails and saddle-
bags.   Contrast with this a fair lady's mode of
travelling in the present day.   She drives with
her man and maid, and three or four well-filled
portmanteaus, to Euston Square or Paddington

Station. The servant gets the tickets and tips
the porter, who sees the luggage properly labelled
and stowed away—and places the lady and her
maid by themselves in a convenient carriage.
Four or five hours bring her to the station nearest
her place of destination. Her friend's carriage is
waiting, and a light van for the luggage. On
arriving at the house she has a nice talk with her
friends before the dressing-bell rings; and when
she goes up to her room she finds her toilet
arranged, and her dresses laid out as smooth and
unruffled as if they were in her own room at Bel-
gravia or Grosvenor Square. I think our Professor might make out an undeniable case of the
superiority of modern travelling over that of our
forefathers.

But some will say, what you have described is
only tip-top civilization—the *crème de la crème*.
Well, think only of the luxury which the hum-
blest classes may enjoy—six hours at the sea-side
for half-a-crown—a trip to the Crystal Palace—
or even a penny steamer. Unquestionably, as
regards travelling, the advantage is all on the side
of the moderns. I am not quite so sure whether,
when the working man gets back after his cheap
trip, he finds his home and its accompaniments
more comfortable than the homes of the same
class were four or five centuries ago. Let this,
however, pass for the present.

But I think I hear an objector say, "You do not treat the subject seriously enough. The value of science does not consist only in these mere personal comforts—there are higher and deeper thoughts connected with the vastness of the discoveries of modern science." I quite agree with this statement, and must apologize for having treated the subject rather too lightly. I would rather base my admiration of science on the sentiment of the Psalmist,—"When I consider Thy heavens, even the work of Thy fingers, the moon, and the stars which Thou hast ordained : What is man that Thou art mindful of him, and the son of man that Thou visitest him? . . . O LORD, our Governor, how excellent is Thy Name in all the world." This is the true spirit in which the man of highest intelligence and piety must view the wonderful works of GOD. Humility and reverence are the right feelings which should be called forth. And every discovery of science, rightly appreciated, should add to these sentiments. Not only the wonderful discoveries in astronomy—the mechanism of the solar system, and, as far as is ascertained, of the starry firmament—the laws by which the Creator governs the vast universe; but, almost more forcibly, the minute arrangement of animal and vegetable life —the inconceivable skill with which the sustentation and continuance of organized life is provided for—the chemical agencies and forces by which, under the government of GOD, the universe is regulated—every new discovery, the greatest as well as the most minute, ought to fill us with increasing gratitude and admiration for the Great Ruler and Creator of all things.

This is the true use of science. If the contemplation of GOD's works fills us, as it should, with love and admiration for the Great Creator of all things, and so leads us to devote ourselves to His service, then we shall have derived from science the true benefit which it was calculated to convey. We should ask ourselves, Are *we* better men, better Christians, humbler, purer, holier, more honest, more religious, more likely to go to Heaven?

But *has* this been the case in the recent enlargement of science? has it made men humbler, more religious, more devoted to GOD? Let us hope it has in some cases; but I fear not in all. I fear that too many minds have been led away from the truth by those very discoveries which should have filled them with wonder and adoration. To what are we to attribute the present flood of impiety and unbelief but, in a great measure, to the abuse of the discoveries which GOD has enabled us to make in His works. The tracing up of secondary causes has led many to deny the existence of a First Cause : the wonderful regularity

of the operations of nature has had the effect of
closing the eyes of too many to the need of a
Ruler, and Governor of the universe; the discovery of laws has, strange to say, blinded some
to the fact that there must needs be some power
to uphold law—that law has no power of operation
by itself, without the constant intervention of an
executive. The beautiful minuteness of organic
life has even been distorted by some, to the monstrous supposition that life is, so to speak, self-
creative. Heresies like these have come to be
received amongst the more rash and speculative
of our philosophers; and I am sorry to say that
some, of whom one might have hoped better things,
have not come forward with the zeal and prompti-
tude with which they should, to repudiate and
disavow the wrong conclusions at which their
brother philosophers have arrived.

If then it be asked, are we the better for the
recent discoveries of science? it is rather difficult
to answer with truth. For if science has led men
to deny their GOD and SAVIOUR, despise His Revelation, and has caused the eternal ruin of souls
for whom CHRIST died, it would be hard for a
Christian not to say that we are the worse rather
than the better—that we have turned to our destruction gifts conferred on us for holier uses.

Look at the question in a national point of
view. It is true that the most wonderful and

D

noble discoveries have been made by modern
science, and springing from them the most excellent improvement in art.   All the beautiful inventions of modern days which adorn our life, all
those useful objects which so much distinguish
the times in which we live—the steam engine
with its multifarious uses, the photograph, the
electric telegraph, and a thousand other ingenious
inventions depend more or less on science.   Very
thankful ought we to be to the great GOD who
has given these things for the embellishment of
our life.   But then again comes the important
question, are we better, better men, better Christians, for all these discoveries?   Compare the present state of society with those which have gone
before—a century ago, two centuries, or say three
centuries ago, in the reign of Queen Elizabeth.
Are Englishmen, as a nation, in a better condition
than at the time when that Queen summoned her
forces to resist the Spanish Armada?   Are our
statesmen better than those who then ruled the
nation ; are our upper classes more noble and
high-minded—less luxurious, effeminate, self-indulgent; are our merchants more noted for integrity and honour ; are our working-men more
sober, industrious, honest ; our women purer, less
vain and frivolous?

    It is very difficult to compare one age with an-
other.   There is a great deal that is good in the

present state of society, but also a great deal that
is very bad.

But how is science involved one way or another
in this state of things? I have already shown
that science viewed as a theory has in some minds
been productive of grievous ill, by shaking the
faith of its professors, which enormous evil has a
good deal permeated society even to its lowest
classes. The press, with its universal agency,
conveys the cavils of the atheist down to the lowest
grades of life. Consider also the effect on the
nation of science as the parent of art—the promoter of all the wonderful discoveries, the conveniences and elegancies of life, which are distributed everywhere, not in England only, but
throughout the habitable globe. Yes, think of
the influence which science has had on "England's commercial prosperity!" The promotion
of our manufacturing system which is the cause
of the conglomeration of our population in over-
grown towns, London and its three millions of
inhabitants, the crowding together of poor miserable families, the wretched homes, the consequent
resort to beer-shops and gin-palaces, the language
and discussion held therein, the state of moral
feeling engendered, the unions, the strikes, the
end of the strikes, and who can tell what that will
be? It is true that we have to set against these
evils, the fortunes of the millionaires, their luxu-

rious houses, their parks, and wide domains—
equal to those of the mediæval aristocrat—their
encouragement of art.   Nor must we forget to
take into our estimation the hundreds and thousands of well-to-do families living in peace and
comfort, dependent mainly on our commercial
prosperity.   But if we set down these more pleasant results mainly to the score of art and science,
it would be unfair, and only deceiving ourselves
to shut our eyes to the enormous evils of the great
towns, with their sweltering population, mainly
the creation of the same causes.

The simple truth is, that the value of our arts
and science has been much neutralized and spoiled.
Science is one of GOD's greatest gifts to man, but
it has been shamefully abused.   First it has been
abused by its recreant professors to the worst uses
of Atheism, whereby the souls of thousands are
in danger of being lost for ever.   Secondly, it has
been in part the source of a state of things, socially
and politically, which has been suffered to run
out into the most hurtful and dangerous excesses.
But there is no real cause for these evils.   They
do not belong to science itself, but to the abuse
of it.   A belief in GOD and in His Fatherly care
is not inconsistent with science, but quite the
contrary.

True science magnifies the power and wisdom
of the great Creator and Father of mankind.   Let

but religious men of science consider the reproach
which is brought on the profession by the unhappy conduct of a few among them, and let
them boldly profess themselves believers in GOD
and His SON JESUS CHRIST, and a better feeling
might be kindled.   Instead of contributing to the
destruction of the souls of men and the ruin of
their country, as the infidels of the last century
did in France, they might be the means of infus-
ing a new life into our effete society, and doing
honour to the Name of GOD.

I am going to make a very bold assertion—but
one that I think can hardly be denied.   I would
say that in comparison with the work done by a
good priest in one parish of England, the whole
work of philosophy is as nothing, except so far as
it leads men to glorify GOD.   The one relates
only to things temporal, the other bears on things
eternal.   The relative value therefore is as time
compared with eternity.

But why make such comparison?   The true
and righteous course would be to link religion
and philosophy together in harmonious action,
and employ both for the highest interests of mankind.

Since writing the above I have read the report
of the doings of the British Association [for
Science] at Bradford.   Great interest was ex-

cited by the lecture of Professor Ferrier on the
" Localization of the Functions of the Brain."
Formerly it was imagined that the brain acted as
a whole, that its functions were wholly intellectual, and that it was impossible to assign special
functions to special parts.   But this notion has
been corrected by recent experiments.   " Nearly
a hundred animals of all classes—fish, frogs, fowls,
pigeons, rats, guinea-pigs, rabbits, cats, dogs, and
monkeys—have been operated on. The plan was to
remove a portion of the skull, and keep the animal
in a state of comparative insensibility by chloroform.   So little was the operation felt that a
monkey, with one side of his skull removed, had
been known to awaken out of his state induced
by chloroform and proceed to catch flies and eat
bread and butter."   The mode of proceeding with
the animals was to apply the electrode to the external convolution of the brain, which was found
to affect the extremities in a remarkable manner.
For instance, if the electrode was applied to the
right side of the brain the animal would kick out
with his left leg, and vice versâ.   Other strange
phenomena were caused by the operation on the
brain.   I cannot help fancying, however, that the
peculiarity of the left side being affected by the
right part of the brain, and vice versâ, is no new
discovery.   For, if I mistake not, the same phenomenon was explained by Dr. Kidd in his lectures

which I attended at Oxford some fifty years
ago. However, I may be mistaken.

"The compliments paid to Dr. Ferrier were
many, and a confident hope was generally expressed that we were on the threshold of discoveries which would make an era in our psy-
chological knowledge." Dr. Crichton Browne
"thought that it was a matter of congratulation
to many present that experiments of so valuable a character had originated in the West
Riding."

I dare say it may be so. Dr. Ferrier seems to
be one of the most intelligent and persevering of
his class, and I believe that the particular department which he has undertaken is considered by
philosophers to be one of great importance.

The reason of my adverting to the subject is
to contrast the work of the philosopher with the
work of the priest. The philosopher has gained a
great triumph if he has shown in what way the
material organization of the brain affects the
other parts of the body. The office of the priest
is so to affect the spirit of man, through the con-
siderations offered to his mind, as to change his
character from sin to holiness—to win him from
the power of evil to the love of GOD. It is the
priest's duty to analyze all the feelings and affections of the human heart, and lead immortal
beings to heaven and happiness.

It is not my wish to disparage the pursuits of
the philosophers; far from it.   Rightly conducted in the fear of GOD they are high and
noble.   All I wish to show is, that the work of
GOD's minister is as far nobler than that of the
philosopher as the immortal spirit of man is
superior to the mere perishable molecules which
constitute the material substance of the brain.

Note.—The following is from the *Christian Observer* of
April, 1823, p. 254.

"M. Flourens has, by a course of experiments on various
animals, accumulated a variety of facts in order to ascertain
that precise part of the brain in which the impressions made
by external objects on the senses centre and produce sensations; and from which other nerves, under the control of the
will, conduct irritation to the muscles, and cause them to perform the movements of the body which have been willed,"
&c.

CHAPTER IV.

WHEN one has occasion to express an un-
favourable opinion of certain members of a class
or profession, it is not reasonable that one should
be accused of condemning the whole class as a
body. There are good and bad servants, good
and bad lawyers, doctors, priests : so there are
good and bad philosophers. If I feel it my duty
to reprove a bad servant, it does not follow that I
consider servants as a class to be "the greatest
plague of life ;" if I object to a bad doctor, think
him stupid, ill-informed, or it may be over-clever
and speculative, disposed to make experiments on
his patients, and caring more for some pet theory
of his own than for their health and comfort, this
is no proof that I have a bad opinion of doctors
generally and of medical science. On the contrary, according to the advice of the Preacher, I
may "honour the physician with the honour due
to him,"[1] and believe that "the LORD hath

[1] Ecclus. xxx. 1.

created him" for the good of mankind. So with
regard to philosophers, I may believe that GOD
hath created them for the good of the human
family, has given them great and valuable qualities, power of thought and discrimination, and
wonderful perseverance; and I may believe that
science itself is a noble thing, calculated to raise
to the utmost the capabilities of the human mind,
and be productive of great benefits to the age in
which it flourishes. And yet with all this, I may
think that some philosophers have greatly mis-
used their gifts, have not realised the uses for
which they were created, have obscured and
thrown back real knowledge instead of advancing
it, have followed some vain fancy of their own
instead of Nature's Great Truth, and consequently
have done evil instead of good in their generation.
The misfortune is, that if the Clergy or Christians
generally express their disapprobation of some of
the notions of modern men of science, they are
immediately charged with prejudice against science
generally, bigotry, intolerance, and so forth, and
the everlasting story of Galileo is thrown in their
teeth, as if there were any parallel between the
persecutors of that ill-treated philosopher and
the compliments and adulations which in the
present day fall to the lot of the admired and
fêted philosopher.

There are philosophers and philosophers, that

is certain. There are some who well deserve all
the honour which has been bestowed upon them,
men who have enlarged the boundary of human
knowledge, opened a way to the investigation of
GOD's works, and deserve well of the generation
in which they live. The great Sir Isaac Newton,
who of all men, perhaps, made the greatest advance in philosophy, was as his biographer records, " thoroughly persuaded of the truth of
Revelation, and amidst the great variety of books
which were constantly before him, that which he
studied with the greatest application was the
Bible. So far from countenancing the atheistical
opinions of certain modern philosophers, he declares his belief that " GOD governs all things,
not as the soul of the world, but as LORD over
all. . . . He is eternal, infinite, absolutely perfect . . . a living intelligent powerful Being . . .
Eternal, Infinite, Omniscient, and Omnipotent."
He wrote a book called " Observations on the
Prophecies of Daniel and S. John ;" and, amongst
other things, " he shewed the exact duration of
our SAVIOUR's ministry upon earth by a strict
demonstration—a difficulty which had mocked the
efforts of the best wits before him." Hear this,
ye scorners of the present day ! Think of the
greatest philosopher of the age, rather of any age,
devoting his time and his thought to these sacred
subjects ! Nor have there been wanting good

Christians among the leading philosophers of the present age—nay, let us hope, they are not exceptions—Sedgwick, Faraday, Buckland, and the other writers of the "Bridgewater Treatises,"—all devoted their high talent to the elucidation of the agreement between Science and Revelation. I quite approve of almost every word in the following extract from the address of the Chairman at the late Medical Congress:

"There existed," he said, "in the minds of all the profession a conviction that science possesses a certain intrinsic value not dependent on its immediate applicability to useful ends. Every day they like other men, were becoming more and more convinced that it was a desirable thing to search after truth by the observation of nature—that those who occupied themselves in this pursuit were substantial benefactors of their country and of the human race. . . . . If he were to attempt to illustrate this he should have to turn to other subjects than those which they had before them, he should have to seek for examples among the professors of those sciences which were sufficiently advanced to be brought into practical application. When he thought of a life like Faraday's, every year of which brought a new accession of knowledge, and, in the end, enriched this country to such a degree as ought to secure him the posthumous adoration of all Mammon-worshippers,

however little they thought of him when alive;
and when he compared the results of Faraday's
life with the life itself, with the contracted labora-
tory in which he laboured, with the mean salary
on which he lived, with his quiet devotion to
science, with the constancy of his religious faith,
and finally with the end of that life—mind and
body exhausted in work, how great in such a man
did that insatiable spirit of inquiry seem, which
found its constant and all-sufficient pleasure in the
discovery of new truth—in wresting from Nature
her secrets by strenuous intellectual efforts."

Unhappily there are other men of science who
have taken a different course. Instead of promoting that "light and sweetness" which is the
characteristic of Christian Truth, they have
abused their high talents to the promulgation of
darkness and bitterness, casting doubts on all that
Christians hold most sacred, and provoking a
spirit of acrimony instead of kindness. What is
a Christian to do with reference to such persons?
Is he to flatter and compliment them, and applaud their cleverness when they are doing all in
their power to frustrate and counteract what he
verily believes to be the greatest possible good?
The Christian is persuaded that the eternal welfare of his own soul and the souls of those around
him depends on their accepting the salvation
which CHRIST has purchased for them: he believes

that the welfare of society, the prosperity of his
country, and all that he holds dear, the happiness
of the whole human race depends on their living
according to the pure and holy law of CHRIST—
that if the nation should reject the true worship
of GOD certain ruin would fall upon it.   He sees
recent evidence of the tremendous evils of infidel
principles in the devastation and misery which
have so lately afflicted France, when but for a few
weeks or months irreligion gained the upper
hand; and it was worse, much worse, at the end
of the last century.   But the philosophical unbeliever seems to care for none of these things.
Apparently he has not the slightest concern for
the soul of his neighbour—if his neighbour has a
soul : and by his rejection of Christianity he casts
in his lot with the Communists and Revolution-
ists, and contributes mainly to the spread of the
worst opinions and principles.   How can the
Christian do otherwise than entertain great suspicion and distrust of such men as these ?   "What
concord hath CHRIST with Belial? or what part
hath he that believeth with an infidel?"   It is not
that unbelievers of the present day are simply unhappy men, much to be pitied, who have missed
the way of salvation; but they are actively mischievous, engaged in doing all in their power to
lead others away from the path of life.

Again, the Christian is persuaded that the only

way of bringing up the rising generation in good
and honest ways is to educate them from their
earliest infancy in the true principles of CHRIST.
With this object he tells his children as soon as
they are able to learn, of the goodness of GOD in
making them His sons and inheritors of His
kingdom. He teaches them the Articles of the
Christian Faith, carefully instructs them in GOD's
commandments, teaches them how to pray; and
what he believes to be most necessary for the welfare
of his own children, he deems it both just and right
to communicate to the children of his poorer neighbours. He thinks it would be mean and selfish
to bring up his own children in the true doctrines
of salvation and take no heed whether the children
of his poorer neighbours are taught the truths or
not. Hence the vast exertions which the clergy
and their friends have made in the past and present generation, while others have made but slight
efforts, to build and maintain schools for religious
as well as secular education. Hence you see in
almost every parish a school connected with the
church, in which the children are brought up to
fear and worship GOD. And hence the personal
exertions which the parish priest makes to instruct
the children under his spiritual charge. But the
unbeliever, caring for none of these things himself, consistently discourages all endeavours to
give religious instruction to the young, and

strange to say, such is the unwholesome compli-
cation of political interests, that in spite of the
wide-spread opinion that education without religion is of no value—nay, cannot properly be called
education at all—the unbeliever has done, and is
doing, much to thwart the endeavours of good
men to imbue the youthful mind of the nation
with the principles of CHRIST's true religion.
How can a Christian have sympathy or fellowship
with men who promote and act on principles
like these—not content to live without GOD
themselves, but perversely doing all they can to
frustrate the labours of GOD's servants to communicate to the poor helpless children of the
nation the knowledge of the way of life?

There is one topic comprised in this argument
which is so intimately connected with the personal
well-being of each individual amongst us, and so
important in every way, that I must not attempt
to discuss it at the end of a chapter, but must
reserve it for one by itself. I mean of course the
different views which the believer and the infidel
take of the duty and efficacy of prayer.

Meanwhile, considering the intense difference
which I have already pointed out between the
advocates of the two principles, it seems obvious
to me that Christian men and women should not
scruple to show a marked discrimination in their
estimate of the Christian philosopher who is living

in the faith and fear of GOD, and is the instrument of exhibiting GOD's glory in His wonderful works, teaching men to look from Nature up to Nature's GOD, and those unhappy and misguided persons whose chief delight seems to be to cast doubts on GOD's Revealed Truth, and lead all with whom they have influence literally to live without GOD in the world. I wonder that right-minded philosophers themselves do not see the necessity of separating themselves from the false brethren who bring so much discredit on their common profession, besides the incalculable mischief which they are sowing broadcast in the world around.

And in making these observations I utterly disclaim, by anticipation, any charge which may be made against me of having said one word which can be justly taken as derogatory either to science itself or to those good men who pursue it in the fear of GOD.

CHAPTER V.

IMMENSELY important as science must be allowed to be by those who have entered at all into the subject—nay, even by those who know science only by the many temporal and worldly advantages which have resulted from it, and are continually advancing the civilisation of the world,—much as we must all admire the ability and perseverance of the philosophers of the present age who have added so wonderfully to the fabric of science, yet it would be untrue to deny that there are some black sheep among them, men who have brought discredit to their high profession, and done infinite mischief by setting science in unnatural and unholy opposition to the Eternal Word of GOD's Revelation. In particular, I adverted in my last letter, to those who have prostituted their talents by disparaging and contradicting those sacred truths by which only, we believe, men can attain happiness either in this world or

in the next : those who oppose themselves to the
charitable work of God's servants in their endeavours to train up the rising generation to be good
and religious men and women. It is a most
grievous thing to see men of ability and perseverance doing all in their power to frustrate what
we Christians believe to be the very highest of all
temporal or eternal interests. The truth is, as I
said before, that philosophers,—some philosophers
I mean,—have no notion of the value of souls,—
in fact, do not believe that man has a soul to be
saved. Their whole system is tainted with this
false error.

There is one especial point which must bring
this subject home to our hearts and consciences.
If there be any doctrine or principle of true
religion more intensely practical than another it
is the necessity and efficacy of prayer. It is not
too much to say that the very object of our creation,—the reason of our being placed upon this
earth,—was that we should be worshippers of
God. God willed that there should be an intelligent race of beings who should be able to understand and acknowledge His infinite goodness
and power, and should render Him a constant
and intellectual adoration, should praise Him
for His greatness, and look to Him as their
FATHER and Preserver, and pray to Him continually for the supply of their temporal and

spiritual necessities. What Christian does not know and acknowledge the value of prayer? Who, when tempted to sin, has not experienced the help and comfort of lifting up his heart to God, and praying for the assistance of the HOLY SPIRIT to aid him in his infirmities? Who that believes in GOD has not, when in trouble and affliction, besought his Heavenly FATHER to comfort and relieve him, and has not felt his soul revived by the kindly influence of the HOLY SPIRIT of Grace strengthening, comforting, refreshing him? Who has not instinctively besought GOD for the recovery of a dear child, or wife, or parent, lying on the bed of sickness?

But now there are men calling themselves philosophers who, knowing nothing of these things themselves, endeavour to shake the faith of GOD's servants in these most holy and consolatory duties; and so would cut them off from the most valuable of all privileges, deprive the afflicted of the sweetest consolation in trouble, rob the sinner of his only hope of being reconciled to GOD, and obtaining pardon and salvation. What are we to think, what are we to do with regard to men who thus labour with a malicious perseverance to undo the work which the HOLY SPIRIT is accomplishing in the hearts of men, prejudicing poor perishing sinners against the only means open to them of obtaining pardon

and peace? I can only say that unless the work
of these men be mere folly and childishness, it is
the most gratuitously cruel and hardhearted thing
which I ever remember to have been done by
civilised men. The whole thing appears to me
such a breach of charity, such an exhibition of
thoughtless selfishness, as has scarcely been exhibited in recent times.

Consider only the naked case. In the midst of
a civilised and Christian community we have sud-
denly brought before us a proposal to test the value
of prayer, by all of us praying during three or four
years for the patients in some particular hospital,
and not praying for some others, and then seeing
in what hospital the greatest number recover!
Was there ever so preposterous a notion,—to test
the goodness and power of GOD by the contemptible experiments of human science, as if scientific
experiments were the one only source of human
knowledge! One can hardly believe that the
propounder of this absurd scheme can be in
earnest. The next thing one would expect him
to do would be to offer to bet a ten pound note
on one of the hospitals against the other. The
one proposal is not one whit more extravagantly
unbecoming than the other. It has surprised me
very much that Clergymen of ability, or any
others, should take the trouble to reply seriously
to this cavil. The "Philosophy of Prayer" for-

sooth! Why, we pray to GOD simply because
GOD has invited and commanded us so to do. If
there is any other duty on which our LORD
JESUS CHRIST and His Apostles insist more than
another, it is the duty of prayer. " Ask and ye
shall have,—seek and ye shall find." " Pray
without ceasing." " Men ought always to pray
and not to faint." " The effectual fervent prayer
of a righteous man availeth much." " Watch
and pray, that ye enter not into temptation." " I
will that men pray everywhere,—lifting up holy
hands." " Is any one among you afflicted,—let
him pray." " The prayer of faith shall save the
sick."

" I have no doubt," the objector will say, " that
all these texts are to be found in Scripture about
the duty and necessity of prayer, but I want
some tangible proof that prayer has really been
effectual." Well, I can give you plenty of instances,—Abraham prayed to GOD, and GOD
healed Abimelech; When Moses prayed to GOD
the fire was quenched. Many times Moses
prayed for the people, and obtained GOD's mercy.
Hannah prayed for a child, and GOD granted her
request. Elisha prayed to GOD, and He restored
the Shunammite's son to life. Elijah prayed for
rain, and it rained abundantly. Hezekiah prayed,
and the LORD added to his life fifteen years.
He prayed again, and GOD sent His destroying

angel, and cut off the hosts of his enemy. Even when the impious Manasseh prayed, GOD was entreated of him and spared him. Job, Jeremiah, Jonah, Daniel, all prayed, and obtained their petitions. Monica prayed for her son Augustine, and he became one of the most eminent Fathers of the Church. The following is a recent example, and, I believe, is an instance of what happens continually. A mother had a wayward, obstinate child whom she could not manage. Punishment and coaxing were alike unavailing. At last a pious friend asked her if she ever prayed for the child. She took the hint, and from that time her child began to amend.

"But," says the objector, "almost all these instances are taken from the Bible; besides it is impossible to tell whether what happened was an answer to prayer, or may have come to pass accidentally. I do not admit the force of these Scriptural examples." "Do you not?" I answer, "that is unfortunate. We Christians do admit these instances as of undoubted certainty. Why should I give up a line of argument which I consider to be absolutely conclusive? As for your proposed test about the hospitals, pardon me for saying it, I look upon it as absolutely silly,—and if not silly, simply profane."

The truth is, that the question rests on GOD's Revelation. I believe in the duty and efficacy of

prayer, because my GOD and SAVIOUR has commanded and encouraged me to pray. I believe
in His authority, on account of the mighty works
which He wrought, the holy doctrines which He
taught, the prophecies which He fulfilled, and
the moral revolution which He has effected.
If you admit none of these things, I do not see
how there is any common ground to argue on.
We have to begin with the question of the truth
of the Bible. Being myself satisfied on this
point, I believe, without a question, that prayer
is the highest duty and privilege of Christians.
When you have disproved the authority of the
Bible, then will be the time to resort to your
philosophical experiments. But until you have
done this, it would be mere childishness to argue
the point on any other hypothesis. I might as
well accept a challenge to a pugilistic contest with
my right hand tied behind me.

The difficulty is to imagine what could possibly
induce a man, the foremost in his proper work,
to travel out of his province and beyond his
depth, in setting himself up to discuss the question of prayer,—if indeed there can be any question about it. How could a man whose whole
soul is set upon matters of earthly science dare to
undertake the tremendous responsibility of unsettling men's minds on the sacred subject of prayer?
When a philosopher undertakes to read us an

amusing and interesting lecture about heat or
light, it is not necessary that we should inquire
what are his religious opinions. But then, on
the other hand, men of science ought to keep to
their own department. It is much more unbecoming for these men of science to intrude their
crude opinions into matters of religion, than for
religious men to criticise their views of science.
A man may be thoroughly competent to explain
the theory of heat to an admiring audience, and
yet be lamentably ignorant of the value and
efficacy of prayer. To make blunders about
science is of temporal interest: to shake the faith
of wavering Christians in the efficacy of prayer,
and so perhaps be the means of many souls
perishing everlastingly, is a fearful responsibility
which no right-minded man would venture on.

There is a common fallacy with regard to this
subject to which before concluding this chapter I
would advert. The scientific sceptic assumes that
when a good man prays for rain or sunshine, or
any other thing connected with what he calls
natural causes, he asks GOD to alter the course
of nature, which he imagines to be impossible.
But this is not necessarily the case. We pray
that GOD will do, only on a larger scale, what we
do for ourselves every day. If our flower-beds
are burnt up by the sun, we use our watering-
pots, and give them a refreshing shower; if we

wish to make our grapes or pineapples ripe we place them in a forcing house. What then can be more natural than to pray to God to send us timely rain or sunshine if we fear lest our crops may be injured by the drought or moisture? We do not pray Him to alter Nature's laws in these cases, but to apply them according to His gracious power. Surely it is not superstition to pray to God to do for us on a larger scale what our gardener does every day. Of course God *could* change the laws of Nature, because it was He that gave them, and it is He that upholds them. But we do not ordinarily pray for such things. We do not pray that He would

> " Annihilate both time and space,
> And make two lovers happy."

We do not pray that He will open the windows of heaven and rain loaves of bread for our use. But we pray simply and in faith, as He has commanded us, that He would give us day by day our daily bread.

CHAPTER VI.

VERY different from the tone and language of
some of our prominent philosophers was the opening Address of Dr. Carpenter at the recent meeting of the British Association at Brighton.   Without altogether agreeing with every point in his
able Address, yet we must admit that the ethical
tone was admirable, and I trust may be taken as
the general feeling, not only of the company who
heard him, but of the majority of those who cultivate science.   "There is a great deal," he said,
"of what I cannot but regard as fallacious and
misleading philosophy—' opposition of science
falsely so called'—abroad in the world at the
present time.   And I hope to satisfy you, that
they who set up *their own conceptions* of the or-
derly sequence which they discern in the phenomena of nature, as fixed and determined laws, by
which those phenomena not only *are* within human
experience, but always *have been*, and always *must
be*, invariably governed, are really guilty of the

intellectual arrogance they condemn in the systems of the ancients, and place themselves in diametrical antagonism to those real philosophers, by whose comprehensive grasp and penetrating insight that order has been so far disclosed." "To set up laws as self-acting, and as either excluding or rendering unnecessary the power which alone can give them effect, appears to me as arrogant as it is unphilosophical. To speak of *any* law as regulating or governing phenomena is only permissible on the assumption that the law is the expression of the *modus operandi* of the governing power . . . . When science, passing beyond its own limits, assumes to take the place of theology, and sets up its own conception of the order of nature as a sufficient account of its laws, it is invading a province of thought to which it has no claim, and not unreasonably provokes the hostility of those who ought to be its best friends." This is true philosophy, and the fact of hearing such sentiments expressed by the President of the British Association might give us a confident hope that the unnatural jealousy between science and theology has passed its culminating point, in the preposterous notion of applying experiment to prayer, and that philosophers and theologians may each take their respective lines without interfering with each other.

After thus expressing my high opinion of the

wisdom and moral excellence of Dr. Carpenter, as
exhibited in his opening Address, it may seem
strange that I should proceed to impugn any of
his opinions. But the truth is, that since the
meeting at Brighton, he has thought it right to
publish a paper in the *Contemporary Review* which,
as it appears to me, goes far to neutralize the
good and wholesome effect of his Address. The
impression conveyed to my mind by comparing
the Address with his paper "On Mind and Will
in Nature" is, that his Address did not please
some of his scientific friends—in fact, that he has
had a good "talking-to" about it—and has been
induced to put forth a sort of apology for the
doctrine delivered at Brighton. I am very sorry
that it should be so. The Address seemed to me
admirably suited to bridge over the unnatural
antagonism which has grown up between religion
and science. The essay, on the other hand, appears
to lay down some irreconcilable positions which
believers in the Bible cannot in any way accept.
I am truly sorry to see this symptom, that scientific men so hang together that they can more
readily give up their religion than their science.
Still, as Dr. Carpenter writes in a courteous and
conciliatory manner, and the worst that can be
said of him is, that unconsciously to himself perhaps, he takes the side of science against religion
in his endeavours to reconcile the two, it may be

well to accept him as a champion of the philosophy of the day, and discuss our differences in a calm and candid spirit.

The grand difficulty, however, in all such discussion is the question how far scientific men are willing to accept Revealed Truth and Scriptural argument as valid; or, how far they think themselves authorized in summarily setting aside Scripture, whenever it appears to them to be at variance with science. I cannot say how surprised I was, after reading with so much satisfaction the Brighton Address of Dr. Carpenter, in which he speaks with disapproval of the arrogance of men of science, and blames those who pass beyond their own limits, and allow Science to take the place of Theology, to find him in his essay lecturing theologians, and bidding them consider whether " the conclusions of science are not at least as worthy of their credence as the teachings of certain Ancient Books, which more and more distinctly appear, the more critically they are studied, to be simply the early beliefs of the Hebrew race as to their relations to their Theocratic Head." Dr. Carpenter forgets that those Ancient Books have the sanction of our Divine Master, have been accepted by the Church of all ages, and have been the chief instrument of the civilization of modern days.

The main difficulty in all discussions between

Philosophers and Theologians is, as I said, the question of the authority which is due to Holy Scripture. Philosophers appear to think that when the Bible seems to be opposed to Science, God's Word must at once give way. Theologians would assert just the contrary. Perhaps the true view of the subject is this, that when Science and the Bible appear to disagree, it is a proof that we imperfectly understand one or the other—probably both. Dr. Carpenter in his Essay on "Mind and Will in Nature," advocates the Darwinian theory which is thus stated in his own words: "that the Creator instead of originating each race by a distinct and separate act (the notion commonly entertained) gave to the first created Monad those properties by the continued action of which through countless ages a man would be evolved." This notion he thinks "will come to be viewed as a far grander notion of Creative design, than the idea of special interposition required to remedy the irregular working of a machine imperfectly constructed in the first instance." He makes no exception in the case of man.

I cannot say that I agree with this opinion. Supposing with the Geologists that the earth has in a long succession of ages passed through various forms, that each system of strata has gradually been formed by natural causes, I cannot myself see anything derogatory to the glory of

God that He should from time to time, as the earth was fitted for their reception, have created new races of animals suited for the changed condition of the habitable globe. Of course, what was most likely beforehand is a purely speculative question. But to me I confess the creation of a Monad, from which, without further operation or care on the part of the Creator, all the animal race, with its vast variety and size and shape, should be evolved, does not commend itself as at all a probable or grand idea. The improbability of this notion is expressed with telling irony in the following lines of the poet :—

> " Some say that in the origin of things,
>   When all creation started into birth,
>   The infant elements received a law
>   From whence they swerve not since : that under force
>   Of that controlling ordinance they move,
>   And need not the immediate Hand Who first
>   Prescribed their course to regulate it now.
>   Thus dream they, and contrive to save a God
>   The incumbrance of His own concern, and spare
>   The great Artificer of all that moves,
>   The stress of a continual act, the pain
>   Of unremitted diligence and care,
>   As too laborious and severe a task."

To me I confess the most " grand" idea is to contemplate the great Creator as an Almighty and bountiful FATHER continually providing for the wants of His creatures, and ruling all things by

His continual Will.   The notion of unintelligent
force without will or intellect, a blind necessity, "Creation's eyeless drudge"—so Evolution
might be called—working out the marvels of the
Universe, appears to me altogether a mean and
valueless conception.   Science is magnificent!
Yes, connected with a Creator, a mighty Will,
Infinite Wisdom ruling over a world of sentient
and intelligent beings—but as recognizing a mere
law and unintelligent force or order it is as comparatively contemptible, as matter compared with
spirit.   However, in a question like this *a priori*
argument is not very forcible.   What Dr. Carpenter or what I may think "grandest," or most
probable, is of small account.   We must look to
facts.

Dr. Carpenter thinks that the conclusions which
most philosophers are disposed to accept (such as
the Palæontological Continuity of Organic Life)
ought to be considered by theologians as worthy of their credence.   Well,—but by parity of
reason, facts and doctrines which all theologians
thoroughly believe, (such as the creation of the
world and all that is in it, at several epochs, and
especially the creation of man in the Image of
GOD,) would equally deserve the credence of philosophers.   We must give and take, and I think
the theologians have the advantage; for their
conclusions rest on the Revealed Word of GOD,

F

whereas the dogmas of philosophers are simply the conclusion of their own invention or imagination.

Dr. Carpenter, like most philosophers, has a bad habit of jumping at conclusions. They imagine things in their own minds, and dwell on them and talk about them with their friends, and then assume that they are proved. Professor Huxley declares that he would rather acknowledge his descent from " a good respectable ape" than from savages or evil persons. And Dr. Carpenter adopts the same opinion. " Mr. Edward Fry," he says, " has recently put forth the point in a form in which I entirely concur. Before we cavil at our poor relatives whom Mr. Darwin would put upon us, let us consider for a moment what relatives we are bound to acknowledge. We *cannot deny* our descent from savages, from barbarians of brutal lives . . . . . with such relatives admitted, any great fastidiousness as to our genealogy seems out of place." It is rather a good joke about the "respectable ape," but nothing more than a joke. Any one will see that Dr. Carpenter's argument is mere assumption. Who admits that we are descended from savages? On the contrary, Dr. Carpenter must surely be aware that even his co-philosophers do not agree with him on this point. The Christian believes that GOD created man "in His own image"—that the

first father of our race was highly endowed—that
our second ancestor, Noah, was a man probably
of high culture, "a preacher of righteousness,"
a man acquainted with all the civilization of many
previous ages. We believe that there has always
been a line of civilized men, and that the savages are
those who by their evil habits, or wilful departure
from the truth taught them by GOD, have degraded themselves from the image of GOD in
which they were created. It is marvellous to me
how a man like Dr. Carpenter can coolly take it
for granted that the present nations of the earth
are all descended from savages, when he must be
aware that it is a point in which the large majority
of educated men entirely differ from him.

The Evolution theory, in its full extravagance,
as set forth by Mr. Darwin and accepted by Dr.
Carpenter, is quite destitute of any substantial
proof—it is contrary to reason, contrary to all
probability, contrary to Scripture, contrary to the
testimony of the Church, not built on any induction, but contrary to the phenomena of geology;
in truth, it has no one proof or evidence whatever
to rest on, but is simply the offspring of a diseased
imagination, dwelling continually on an unwarranted hypothesis. That it may not be supposed
that this is the opinion only of a priest who knows
little or nothing of the matter, I will quote a
passage from the pages of one who stands high

among philosophers themselves.   Would there
were many such ! " Straining after the impossible," he says, " we have entered into an age of
speculative philosophy, which bids fair to destroy
all that is high and noble in our conceptions of
nature, and to lead us into the cold unimpassioned
region of scepticism.   To mock all sense of the
beautiful with the derisive laugh of materialism
—to check the aspiration of refined mental culture by the assumption of theories which are revolting to our better nature—to destroy upon
unsound grounds the faith which every man of
nobility of intellect has, and always will have, in
the ever present mind, and thought, and hand of
the Creator in Creation—to replace a final cause
with a self-acting secondary law—to substitute
chance for design, and to patch up a destroyed
faith by attempting to reconcile truth and falsehood—when things have come to such a pass as
this, the strongest mind might tremble for the
fate of science itself, were it not confident in the
ultimate triumphs of the true."[1]   No wonder,
that, as one of the speakers at the Leeds Congress
informed the meeting, " the Academy of Science at
Paris refused to admit Mr. Darwin as a corresponding member of its body, on the ground that

[1] An Exposition of the Fallacies in the Hypothesis of Mr.
Darwin. By C. R. BREE, M.D., F.Z.S., Senior Physician
to the Essex and Colchester Hospital, &c., p. 328.

his work on the *Origin of Species* was thoroughly
unscientific, and was not based upon sound argument, but upon received assumption."

Besides being unscientific, the Evolution theory
is altogether irreligious and contrary to GOD's revealed Word. It excludes all miracles, and so
annuls at once the Old and New Testament. It
does away with the value of prayer. It deprives
poor sinful, suffering man of the consolation and
hope of calling on GOD for relief in his necessities.
It destroys in fact the essence of religion. The
essence of religion is to love GOD. But it is impossible to love a mere law or order, an impersonal
abstraction or "stream of tendency." The idea
is nonsensical. Lastly, it makes the life of this
present world to be all in all. It denies the
miracle of the Resurrection, and the hope of the
world to come. The cruel tyrant who has ruled
with iron sway, and rendered miserable the lives
of thousands, the murderer, the adulterer, the cor-
rupter of female innocence, the selfish Sybarite,
will, according to this heartless creed, suffer no
retribution in the world to come. The poor and
honest man, who has endured much injustice in
this world, the thousands and tens of thousands
of toiling and suffering men who have passed their
days in laborious drudgery, toiling in mines during
a long and painful life, labouring in furnaces and
other unwholesome occupations—and have borne

their hard lot in patience and hope, will die and be no more—instead of being, as the Christian hopes and believes, raised by the power of GOD to the realms of bliss, there to live in joy unspeakable for eternal ages.   All that GOD has given them, according to the Darwinian creed, is a life of toil and suffering here, and at the end— annihilation !

May GOD forgive the philosophers who have promulgated these heartless dogmas, and give them grace to recant their dreary superstition !

It may perhaps need some apology that I should take upon myself to analyze the intellectual workings of a very respectable and highly gifted gentleman.   Dr. Carpenter is a representative man, and stands high in the estimation of the scientific world, and is fond, like many others, of publishing his opinions to the world.   I venture therefore to express an opinion on a point of very great importance both to men of science and to others, as to the way in which the former suffer themselves to be deceived much to their own disadvantage, how without intending to sacrifice religious truth they do nevertheless imperceptibly lose their hold on it by incautious admissions and by quite unnecessary sacrifice of points on which the truth depends.   If we admit the being of a GOD, it is surely not more philosophical to suppose that He created a monad and gave to it "those properties by the continual operation of which, through countless ages, a man was evolved," than that He created different races of animals at the time when the earth was prepared to receive them. Philosophically and scientifically it seems to me to make no difference whatever. But religiously it makes all the difference in the world. The former supposition takes away from the Creator all care over His own works, and consequently precludes the necessity of worship and obedience; for why should creatures pay homage to a Being whose sole connection with them was that in ages past He created the germ of life? The admission of this strange notion of an aboriginal speck or monad seems to be a gratuitous rejection of religious truth, without the slightest gain to philosophy. Yet into this snare has a man with Dr. Carpenter's general good principle fallen. He has given way to a false feeling of deference to the very men whom he has before denounced as "arrogant." It is but the case, I fear, with too many others. They are led to admit the possibility of some seductive theory without considering that it costs them their religious faith. They play into the hands of the sceptic and unbeliever, and so throw their influence into the balance not in favour of philosophy, for to philosophy it matters nothing, but simply against the truth.

Men of science, it seems to me, have formed

themselves too much into a clique. In the eager
pursuit of their favourite object and in the constant intercourse with men of their class, they
become so embued with the mode of thinking,
and prejudices, and false assumptions of those with
whom they are brought into contact, that they
incautiously give up vital points, or accept theories, which in regard to philosophy, are not in the
least essential, but only assumed by the more
rash spirits among them; but the giving up or
acceptance of which is in reality a sacrifice of Revealed Truth. Without meaning harm they
make such concessions to the Pantheist and the
Ultra-Evolutionist as, if true, would drive the
Creator from His own Creation and make a God
out of the mere order of Nature.

If it were only philosophers who fell into this
error or inconsistency I should not, perhaps, have
thought it necessary to say so much as I have
done about it—not for want of the desire, if it
might be, to help them in their dire struggle with
the enemy of souls, but simply from diffidence as
to my power to influence them. But the same
unhappy principle, or rather want of principle,
has permeated other classes of society. Even
amongst the clergy there are those who have unconsciously fallen into the same error. Unfor-
tunately science has attained a sort of temporary
fashion; its magnificent discoveries have capti-

vated the present generation ; its valuable inventions in art, the conveniences and luxuries which the present age derives from its labours, all these have so impressed the minds of unthinking and even thoughtful men, that they have suffered themselves to be blinded to the dangers which lurk beneath the surface. They have failed to perceive that together with the splendid theories and practical wonders of science, Satan, with his usual skill, has contrived to sow the seeds of evil, to insinuate scepticism and the pride of intellect. What the Christian must aim at is to separate the chaff from the wheat, and learn to discriminate between true and false philosophy; and instead of fancying that he finds in science disproof of an over-ruling Providence, to discover rather increased evidence of the Power, the Wisdom, and Goodness of the great Creator and Ruler of the Universe.

P.S.—Dr. Carpenter, I believe, alludes to a paper of mine in the following passage, printed in the *Contemporary Review* for April, 1873, p. 787 :

" Of the prejudice existing in a certain section of the public mind on these subjects, a very curious example is afforded by the fact that I have lately seen my Paper in this Review, on 'Mind and Will in Nature,' publicly characterized as atheistical, on account of its acceptance of the

Evolution doctrine: the writer expressing great regret that it had entirely destroyed the hopes which my Brighton Address had led him to form."

It certainly does appear to me that the passages in this chapter quoted from Dr. Carpenter's Brighton Address are totally irreconcileable with other passages in the *Contemporary Review* in which he seems to advocate the extremest views of the Evolutionists. How he can reconcile them I am at a loss to discern.

As to what is atheistic and what is not, Philosophers it seems differ from Divines. But to teach that "GOD created a Monad and gave it those properties by the continued operation of which, through countless ages, a man was evolved," when GOD has distinctly told us that on the sixth day, or age, "GOD created man in His own image," I confess appears to me very much like Atheism. The Christian's GOD is an Almighty Intelligent Spirit, Who created the heaven, the earth, the sea, and all that in them is, and not only created them, but rules over them continually, controlling the wills and affections of sinful men, pledged by His sacred Word to punish unrepentant sinners, and to reward with eternal life those who believe in Him and diligently seek Him. To deny this GOD is in my judgment Atheism.

CHAPTER VII.

IT appears to me that many worthy men, who are philosophers, fall, without suspecting, it into grievous heterodoxy from the unwary following the opinions of men not nearly so worthy of credit as themselves. Thus Sir John Lubbock, who writes almost invariably in a just and temperate spirit, is liable to serious objection when he follows the commonplace but unwarranted dogmas of his brother philosophers. In his interesting book on "The Origin of Civilization, and Primitive Condition of Man," after describing the condition of man in his savage state, and relating the strange superstitions, and gross practices into which he has fallen, he proceeds, "Nay, in the absence of education, not even Christianity prevents mankind from falling into these errors. . . . . A belief in witchcraft was all but universal until lately in our own country. This dark superstition has indeed flourished for centuries in Christian countries, and has only been ex-

pelled at length by the light of science." I am
not disposed to deny that science may have had
its effect in dispelling the belief in witchcraft,
though, unless Sir John Lubbock be a believer in
spirit-rapping, he must admit that a belief scarcely
less unscientific has sprung up in its place. But
it is the following passage to which I chiefly desire to draw attention, "The immense service
which science has thus rendered to the cause of
religion, and of humanity, has not hitherto received the recognition which it deserves. Science
is still regarded by many excellent but narrow-
minded persons as hostile to religious truth,
while in fact she is only opposed to religious
error. No doubt her influence has always been
exercised in opposition to those who present con-
tradictory assertions under the excuse of mystery,
and to all but the highest conceptions of Divine
power. The time however is approaching when
it will be generally perceived that so far from
science being opposed to religion, true religion
without science is impossible; and if we consider
the various aspects of Christianity as understood
by different nations, we can hardly fail to perceive
that the dignity, and therefore the truth of their
religious belief is in direct relation to the knowledge of science and of the great physical laws by
which our universe is governed."—P. 256.

These are evidently the words of an earnest

man, who in his love for science yet does not intend to forsake his religion.

But there is a manifest fallacy in the whole argument which I think the writer himself will be disposed to admit when pointed out to him. It is of course undeniably true that true science and true religion must be harmonious with each other,—and that is one chief point which I am desirous of establishing. But then there is a "philosophy falsely so called." There are philosophers and philosophers. I do not think that Sir J. Lubbock gives due weight to this undeniable truth. Again, science is tentative and ever advancing: what is held by many to-day, may be disproved or greatly modified to-morrow. The philosophers of the next century will, we may feel sure, have advanced far beyond those of the present generation. Therefore although we may "admit that true science may be a great aid to religion," yet it seems obvious that there may be much in the present opinions of men of science which may be found to be antagonistic to true religion.

Let us briefly consider some of these points.

From the general tone of Sir J. Lubbock's writings, I think I might venture to infer that he is not a man who denies the value of what Christians believe to be not only the first of duties, but the most efficacious of all means of spiritual advancement, without which no man could for a moment be considered a Christian or religious man. I need scarcely say that I advert to prayer. Now it is notorious that some of the most advanced men of science of the present day doubt, or even deny the value of prayer. It is an evasion of the question to say that they only doubt the value of prayer for rain or fair weather, or even for relief from sickness. They deny the use of prayer altogether. In truth, they deny that there is any personal GOD Who listens to prayer. Will Sir J. Lubbock venture to say that this is an instance of the "immense service which science has rendered to the cause of religion and humanity," and in which, "so far from science being opposed to religion, true religion without science is impossible?" It may be true that science has helped to discourage the belief in witchcraft, but if with witchcraft it has made men doubtful as to the value of prayer, surely Sir J. Lubbock would not consider that we have gained an advantage. He must admit that this is a great drawback to the value of science. Why then does he not take pains to discriminate, and not give the benefit of his unqualified approval to the value of this so-called science of the day?

Again, there can be no doubt that the prevailing atheism and infidelity is due to the rash speculations and crude assertions of some men of science. Of course I do not include all in this

sweeping assertion. In truth, I believe there are
very few who would avow themselves atheists.
They salve their conscience by the notion that
if only they admit the existence of a First Cause,
it is not atheism to deny His governance of the
world and the care of His creatures. They deny
the existence of GOD as a Father, or Ruler of the
universe; and hence arises the depreciation of
the value of prayer. Their notion is that there
is some settled order of things which goes on
without the intervention of a Higher Power,
though they do not deny that there may possibly
have been some Higher Power which first set all
things in motion—some Unknowable First Cause.
Surely Sir J. Lubbock must perceive that this is
a mere fallacy, or at least that it is using terms
in a different sense from what they have always
hitherto been used. What Christians mean by
GOD, nay, what men of any religion mean by
GOD, is a mighty Unseen Spirit Who guides and
governs all things by His power and wisdom.
Can Sir J. Lubbock really think that in the denial
of a GOD, as hitherto believed in by mankind we
have an instance of " the immense service which
science has rendered to the cause of religion and
humanity ?" Surely then he ought to have
qualified his assertion, that " true religion without science is impossible," seeing that the science
of the present day, at least in the hands of some

of its professors, sets itself directly against this very belief in a GOD, depriving suffering man of the hope and comfort of believing himself under the protection of a wise and beneficent Father Who is a Rewarder of those who diligently seek Him.

Take again the denial of miracles, which is another instance of the influence of the so-called science of the present day, so far as it has spread itself amongst the people. Does not he perceive that to deny the possibility of miracles does, at one stroke, cut us off at once from all belief in the Bible, which is simply an inspired narrative of GOD's miraculous intervention in the affairs of the world? Does he really mean to destroy the faith of all Christian people? Does he intend that science should supersede the religion of the best and most enlightened of mankind, no less than the hope and comfort of the poor and afflicted—deprive them of the hope of a reward hereafter, and of the check which religion imposes on the evil deeds of men? Judging from the general tone of Sir J. Lubbock's writings, I should not have said that this was his intention. He seems to speak as Christians generally speak of the superstition and cruelties of heathen nations and of the great superiority of the Christian religion. He cannot then deliberately intend to advocate the advance of that sort of science which

denies a GOD or a Providence, and scoffs at the
notion of a " Good FATHER Who listens to the
prayers of His people."

Again he says, " Fully satisfied that religion
and science cannot in reality be at variance, I
have striven in the present publication ('Pre-
historic Times,') to follow out the rule laid down
by the Bishop of London, in his excellent lecture
delivered last year at Edinburgh. The man of
science, says Dr. Tait, ought to go on 'honestly,
patiently, diffidently, observing and storing up his
observations, and carrying his reasonings unflinch-
ingly to their legitimate conclusions, convinced
that it would be treason to the majesty of science
and of religion if he sought to help either by
swerving ever so little from the straight line of
truth.' " Ah! it were well if all men of science
did thus act "honestly and diffidently."

It is a great misfortune that philosophers, who
are really good men at heart, should be so mixed
up with the speculation of atheists and unbelievers, as to seem not to dare to raise their voice
against them, and vindicate the true value of
science as a gift which a wise and merciful GOD
has bestowed on men, not to supersede but to aid
and confirm the revelation of His Word. For in
truth there is no sort of real antagonism between
them. It is simply an unprovoked attack on religion which some men make in the supposed

G

interests of science. Viewing the matter simply from a philosophical point of view, how does it logically differ whether, as they suppose, things go on of themselves in a settled order, or whether GOD has established a law which cannot be broken —a law which He Himself upholds and maintains? The exceptional occasions on which for His own wise purposes He interferes in the regular operation of that law do not in any perceptible degree affect the discoveries of science.

Could not some society be formed with Sir J. Lubbock and Dr. Carpenter at the head, consisting of philosophers determined to uphold the Christian religion, and set themselves against the aggressions of the infidels?

CHAPTER VIII.

THERE is a remarkable passage at the end of Dr.
Carpenter's recent paper in the *Contemporary Review*, on "Mind and Will in Nature," in which
a contrast is drawn between Pantheism and Anthropomorphism. Anthropomorphism is the at-
tributing to GOD the passions and feelings, and
even form of man. Pantheism is the denial of a
Personal GOD, or as Dr. Carpenter represents it,
"the absence of any distinct recognition of that
conscious volitional agency which is the essential
attribute of personality, without which the universe is nothing else than a great self-acting machine." The truth, as Dr. Carpenter says, lies
between these extreme opinions. The question
with him is as to the point at which the truth is
placed. This is an important matter in the con-
troversy between science and theology, and demands close attention.

Men are led into the error of Pantheism by

fixing their attention too exclusively on the laws
and forces of nature, so as to think of the Divine
Being as the mere first principle of the universe,
and His agency throughout the world as, not the
direction or government, or interference in the
concerns of the creatures which exist, but a sort
of fatal necessity, whereby all things go on from
age to age in a regular sequence without the need
of the controlling intervention of an over-ruling
Providence.   Anthropomorphism, in Dr. Carpenter's view, is the reverse of this.   It may be best
illustrated by examples; but, in truth, Anthropomorphism rightly viewed is really a mere figure
of speech.   It is only when what are mere figures
are supposed to be realities that Anthropomorphism is liable to censure.

There are countless passages in Holy Scripture
in which by a figure of speech the action of man
is attributed to the Deity.   God is said to have
delivered the Israelites from the house of their
bondage " by a mighty hand and outstretched
arm."   But no one surely could suppose that this
was anything but figurative and poetical language.
It is probably on account of the irreverence of
supposing that God can be represented by any
outward form that the ancient Church, like our
own, refrained from making any representation of
the Eternal FATHER, which must needs be derogatory to His dignity.   But in word-painting

there is not the same need of reticence. God is often spoken of in language at once the most sublime and the most hyperbolical. No other language equals the Hebrew in the astonishing sublimity of its conception of the Deity, "He rode upon the cherubims and did fly, He came flying upon the wings of the wind." "Thou deckest Thyself with light as with a garment, and spreadest out the heavens like a curtain. Who layeth the beams of His chambers in the waters, and maketh the clouds His chariot, and walketh upon the wings of the wind." Now, if any persons reading these passages in the Bible supposed that they were to be taken in their exact literal interpretation, of course that would be very bad theology. They are simply passages of the most astonishing magnificence, to be understood as poetical imagery. I question whether Homer, or Pindar, or any other poet has passages of equal grandeur.

But besides these representations of God with visible form and attributes, there are also a great many passages in which He is described as endowed with human feelings and passions, which are to be taken in an Anthropomorphic sense as much as those which represent Him in human or visible form. Thus when it is said that in consequence of the wickedness of man before the flood, "it repented the Lord that He had made

man upon earth, and it grieved Him at the heart,"
or again, when the LORD said, "Because the cry
of Sodom and Gomorrah is great, and because
their cry is very grievous, I will go down now
and see whether they have done altogether according to the cry of it, which is come unto Me,
and if not, I will know." So, when GOD is called
a jealous GOD, and said to be filled with fierce
anger. It is difficult to know precisely where to
draw the line between the figure of speech which
we call Anthropomorphism, and what is reality.
For there is no doubt that GOD did sometimes
appear in bodily form, and that many times His
Voice was heard. But in truth, in most of these
cases, it is not of essential importance whether the
passage is to be considered figurative or not—
because the figure, if it be a figure, is used for the
purpose of giving the clearest impression of the
truth. I scarcely think that in these days any
great error or superstition can arise even from
exaggerated Anthropomorphism. No person except the most ignorant could take in their literal
sense these figures of speech which are used to
illustrate the relation in which we stand to GOD,
and GOD to us. Certainly no intelligent English
Churchman could fall into the error, for the first
of the Thirty-nine Articles begins—" There is but
one living and true GOD, without body, parts, or
passions, of infinite power, wisdom, and goodness :

the Maker and Preserver of all things, both visible and invisible."

No, the danger is altogether on the other side. Scientific sceptics have brought themselves so to contemplate GOD as a mere impersonal force that they would explain away all the literal truth of our religion and bring in a mere scientific atheism. It is remarkable that in the very next paper to that of Dr. Carpenter in the *Contemporary Review* which we have been considering, there is an article that bears on the subject of Anthropomorphism. It is signed "The Author of ' Hints towards a serious attempt to estimate the value of the Prayer for the Sick' "—and is dated from the Athenæum Club, Sept. 1872. Who is the gentleman? Let him explain himself. "I am a physiologist, say, belonging to a section of the ' narrow' physicists—or a geologist. I am engaged in a search after the manner and nature of work exercised by some great power infinitely beyond me. What wonder and admiration overwhelm me, as I trace the operation of a Supreme Intelligence. I may or may not anthropomorphise that Power, and call Him ' Creator,' ' Deity,' 'Father,' what you will." We are not concerned to follow out the argument of this "narrow physicist," as he ironically calls himself, but merely to ascertain what is his view, and that of his brethren, of Anthropomorphism. One meaning o'

Anthropomorphism is, in his view, to call GOD
" Creator," " Father." I am glad that this
illustration has occurred, because it shows, beyond
a question, what is the real meaning of these
philosophers. It is simply the eradication of the
principle of all religion from the soul of man.
No wonder that this writer should doubt the value
of prayer, when he has ceased to regard GOD as
his *Creator* or his *Father.* The very principle of
all religion is to believe that we are placed in the
world by an Almighty and All-wise Creator, who
preserves the creatures which He has made, and
loves them as a father loves his children, and desires nothing so much as their happiness, and
watches over them with a Father's care. All this
we are told is Anthropomorphism, an extreme
view to be avoided as much as Pantheism !

But the truth is, Dr. Carpenter has made a
mistake in classing Pantheism and Anthropomorphism together as forms of religion, or no religion.
Pantheism indeed is a deadly heresy—virtually
the denial of the existence of GOD—but Anthropomorphism is merely a figure of speech. It does
not follow that it is a religion because it ends in
" ism." It is a word like sophism, truism, sole-
cism, vulgarism, and merely designates a mode of
speaking of the Almighty in terms intelligible to
the human mind. This is its real meaning. But
when it is diverted from its true meaning, and

understood as being the same as calling GOD our
Creator or our Father, when such language and
belief as this is repudiated under the name of
Anthropomorphism, it is simply to repudiate the
highest and holiest truths of religion.

Mr. Matthew Arnold in his recent book called
"Literature and Dogma, an Essay towards the
better understanding of the Bible," laments the
wide-spread infidelity which pervades the working classes. "An inevitable revolution," he says,
"of which we all recognise the beginnings and
signs, but which has already spread perhaps far-
ther than most of us think, is befalling the religion in which we have been brought up." I am
not sure of this. We may hope in the first place
that the present infidelity *appears* more con-
spicuously in the present age, because men have
ceased to be ashamed of being infidels. There is
always I fear a vast latent mass of infidelity.
But now men are so bold as to avow it. Hitherto
the truth has always revived. GOD grant it may
do so again. In the last century Voltaire spread
his noxious opinions through France, Tom Paine
corrupted the uneducated classes of this country,
Hume spread his cold scepticism amongst men
of letters. Nor was there wanting a Darwin to
tell us that we were all descended from apes.
Yet all this passed away before the revival of
religion, first under the form of Evangelicalism,

in which respect to the Holy Scriptures was conspicuous. Let us trust that the recently roused energy of the Church may prove more than sufficient to meet the present assaults of sceptics and Latitudinarians.

Mr. Matthew Arnold suggests another method. "To re-inthrone the Bible as explained by our current theology, whether learned or popular, is absolutely and for ever impossible, [he thinks,] as impossible as to restore the predominance of the feudal system, or the belief in witches." No, he has hit upon a better plan,—he proposes to to explain the Bible upon an entirely new system. And what do my readers suppose is his method? Simply to leave out the character of GOD! "The word GOD," he says, "is by no means a term of science, of exact knowledge, but a term of poetry and eloquence, a literary term in short," (p. 12.) "For science," he says, "GOD is simply the stream of tendency by which all things fulfil the law of their being," (p. 41.) He scoffs at the idea that "GOD is a Personal First Cause, Who thinks and loves,—the moral and intelligent Author and Governor of the universe." Now there are many infidels in the present day, many of the character described by the Psalmist, who say in their heart, "There is no GOD." But the peculiarity of Mr. Matthew Arnold is that he admits the inspiration of Holy Scripture, and

yet denies the existence of a "First Cause, the
Author and Governor of the universe." He ad-
mires the Bible very much, the first words of
which are, "In the beginning GOD created the
heaven and the earth," yet he altogether denies
the notion of GOD being our Creator, Father, and
Ruler.

And the way in which he would restore the Bible
to the love and respect of the people is by substituting for the notion that GOD is our Creator and
Father, which He considers anthropomorphic, the
belief that GOD is "the enduring power, not ourselves, that maketh for righteousness," (57 et
passim,) Mr. Arnold insists very strongly on this
point. It is in fact the key-stone of his edifice.
Once get out of people's heads the notion that
the Bible teaches them that GOD is their Maker,
or Father, or Preserver, and substitute for these
errors the belief that all the Bible teaches us in
this matter is the self-evident truth that "the
Eternal is an enduring power, not ourselves, that
maketh for righteousness," and the case will be
quite altered; the people will believe the Bible
again, and follow after righteousness, at least
much more than they do at present.

And this is nineteenth century philosophy!

CHAPTER IX.

THERE is a strange fallacy current among sceptics, that because some people profess one religion
and some another, no one has a right to say that
his religion is the best. "Whether you be a
Christian, a Moslem, a Hindoo, a Buddhist, a
Parsee, or a Fetish-worshipper," you are equally
debarred from assuming that your religion is
better than that of others.

Now this is contrary to the practice of men in
every other department of knowledge or practice.
There can be but one nearest road from one place
to another; all others must be wrong, or at least
roundabout. In casting up a sum only one total
can be right. Suppose several persons want to
know the exact time, they all take out their
watches and find them different, yet only one
can be correct. One person perhaps says "I am
sure mine must be right, for I set it this morning
at the station." The others having no such evidence to show probably acquiesce. I admit that

in respect to different Churches, or different schools of opinion in the Church, there is some truth in this theory. All professing Christians believe that the Word of GOD is contained in Holy Scripture, and accept the Creeds as the summary of their faith ; but some schools in the Church dwell more on one aspect of the Truth than others, and so, to a certain extent, all may be true, at least partially. But when you speak of entirely different religions,—Christian, Buddhist, Fetish-worship,—it is clear that only one can be true, the rest must needs be false. A story is told of the bronze statue of S. Peter, at Rome, which is an object of great reverence to pilgrims and others, but is said by some to have been originally a statue of Jupiter. A young Englishman, rather profanely it must be confessed, knelt down and kissed the foot of the image, saying, " O, good Jupiter, if your turn ever comes round again remember me, I pray you, that I did not, like others, neglect you in your misfortunes." This is on the principle of scepticism. Who knows whether Jupiter and Juno, or Thor and Wodin, or Vishnu and Siva may not be the true deities after all ? How can we Christians believe that we are right and everybody else wrong ?

In the first place, Christian nations are the most advanced and enlightened people in the world. We do not pay this mock deference to

other people in other matters. We feel and know
that in civilization we are the superior. We do
not for a moment suppose that the Fetish-wor-
shippers of the Fiji Islands are equal to us in other
things. Why should we imagine it possible that
their Fetish-worshipping should be possibly as
good as Christianity?

But the fact is, that no other religion in the
world has any evidence to show for its truth.
No evidence whatever could be brought forward
by the worshippers of Zeus and Here that there
ever were such gods or people at all. Socrates
said jocosely, that he supposed that people must
know who were their ancestors, alluding to those
who supposed themselves to be descended from
the gods. No other proof could be given. But
in the case of Christianity, we know that there is
an immense body of evidence which has been
thoroughly sifted and accepted by the ablest and
most intellectual men. Nothing of the sort can
be alleged with regard to other religions.

Now I do not mean to say that it is necessary
for all persons to go through this process of
searching into evidence. Thousands there are who
are quite incompetent to weigh the evidences of
Christianity. Multitudes have been baptized into
CHRIST'S Church, and never entertained a doubt
of the truth of their religion. The cavils of
sceptics appear to them to have no weight. Still

it is important in these days, to be able to give a reason for the faith that is in us. We are living in critical times, not unlike the middle of the last century. My hope and belief is, that the influence of pseudo-Philosophy has done its worst—that the Darwin bubble, especially the ape hypothesis, will soon explode, as the similar fancy of Lord Monboddo and the elder Darwin did in the last century. Educated persons are, I trust, beginning to discern that this style of attack on religion is simply the going back to follies which have long since been refuted; in fact, they are but the resuscitation of Pagan Philosophy.

Meanwhile, it behoves all those to whom Truth is dear to bestir themselves vigorously in bearing testimony against the cavils and delusions which are abroad. For, though we may entertain no doubt that Truth will in the end prevail, yet it is to be feared that many individuals may be led astray and ruined. It is important, therefore, that each person should be able, if exposed to attacks, as almost every one is more or less, to have at hand convincing answers to the cavils which abound. I do not propose in this, or any following paper, to supply a regular treatise on Evidence,[1] but rather advert to some of the most prominent cavils which present themselves in the present day.

---

[1] I have endeavoured to do this in some degree at least in a work recently published and placed on the list of the S.P.C.K called "Thoughts on the Bible."

And first I wish to point out a mistake which is not unfrequently made by some very good men. All Christians, I suppose, have their peculiar ground of belief—their own special reasons or influences which have satisfied their own minds. What I think is unwise, is that very able writers, arguing with convincing eloquence on some particular branch of evidence, are too apt to disparage other lines of argument which have appeared to other minds as convincing as their own favourite thoughts have to themselves. This is ill-advised, because these writers are mutually refuting each other. One man, for instance, shall dwell mainly on the miracles of our LORD, or the prophecies as evidences of His mission. Another shall rest his faith on the testimony of the Church, and shall speak disparagingly of miracles. Another shall dwell exclusively on the testimony of his own conscience and feelings as to the efficacy of faith in CHRIST. He forgets that this testimony is available only to one who is already living in the faith and fear of GOD. Books of evidence, such as Butler's Analogy and Paley's three Treatises on Natural Theology, the Evidences, and the Horæ Paulinæ are mainly intended to influence the minds of those who do *not* believe. They are calculated to remove, if GOD will, and through the operation of the Spirit, the causes of their unbelief. It is most true that the truths of Christianity cannot be demonstrated into people's minds without the aid of the HOLY SPIRIT, but still the arguments

used may be the means by which the HOLY SPIRIT
shall work for the salvation of souls. And besides
affording matter of conviction to unbelievers and
doubters, the consideration of the Evidences of
Religion is eminently fitted for filling the minds
of believers with gratitude and devotion. What
can be more grateful to the mind of a Christian
philosopher than the proof of GOD's wisdom and
goodness summed up in Paley's Natural Theology,
which might be indefinitely increased by the marvels of creation which science has unfolded since
his time? Or take the divine character of our
LORD, or His doctrine, or the progress of His
kingdom; or take Dr. Pusey's book on the Prophet Daniel, or the convincing force of Prophecy
as set forth in his recent Sermons headed "Prophecy, a Series of Miracles which we can examine
for ourselves," "the Prophecy of CHRIST our Inter-
cessor and Atoner in Isaiah liii.," and "CHRIST
the Light of the world, to be rejected by His own,
to be despised, and so to reign in glory." These
various writings not only tend to remove, through
GOD's grace, the difficulties from the minds of imperfect believers, but also build up in the hearts of
believers increased feelings of love and faith. One
form of evidence is more suited to one mind, and
one to another. And hence it would be a mistake
to disparage any one form of evidence because we
ourselves have been struck chiefly by another.

H

pressed of the devil: for GOD was with Him."
Paul also, in his Epistle to the Hebrews, says
at GOD bore them witness "both by signs and
onders, and with divers miracles and gifts of the
OLY GHOST." This evidence of miracles is con-
nually referred to in Holy Scripture. I am at a
ss, therefore, to understand why any one should
cruple to use this argument in the case of those
hose faith is doubtful. The miracles were wrought
xpressly for the more confirmation of the faith.

Having appealed to the mighty deeds and mira-
les of JESUS of Nazareth, S. Peter goes on in his
'entecostal address to refer to the testimony of
rophecy, and specially in confirmation of the
Lesurrection.   " Men and brethren, let me freely
peak to you of the patriarch David," it is not of
limself that he spake when he said, " Thou wilt
lot leave my soul in hell, nor suffer my body
ver to see corruption," but he "spake of the
Lesurrection of CHRIST, that *His* soul was not left
n hell, neither *His* flesh did see corruption."
Here we have the testimony of prophecy as well
is miracles appealed to in the first sermon which
was preached.   Our LORD Himself used the same
argument with the two disciples, on their way to
Emmaus. " Beginning at Moses and all the prophets, He expounded to them in all the Scriptures
the things concerning Himself."

Another sort of evidence which has great weight

with many minds is, not the "mighty deeds,"
but the "gracious words" of JESUS. "Never man
spake like this man." All men wondered at
"the gracious words which proceeded out of His
mouth." "The people were astonished at His
doctrine." How different was the teaching of our
LORD from that of the philosophers of old, and
from the maxims of the ancient world. "Blessed
are the poor in spirit, for they shall be comforted.
Blessed are the meek, for they shall inherit the
earth. Blessed are the merciful, for they shall
obtain mercy. Blessed are the poor in heart, for
they shall see GOD. Blessed are the peacemakers,
for they shall be called the children of GOD. . . .
Take My yoke upon you and learn of Me, and ye
shall have rest for your souls, for My yoke is
easy and My burden is light." The same spirit
breathes in the writings of the Apostles. "Be
kindly affectioned one to another in brotherly love,
in honour preferring one another." See also S.
Paul's exquisite description of charity. Contrast
with this the description of Homer's chief hero—

"Impiger, iracundus, inexorabilis, acer,"[1]

or the boasted policy of Ancient Rome—

"Parcere subjectis et debellare superbos."[2]

While the humble and poor would feel the

[1] Restless and angry, inexorable, fierce.
[2] To spare the conquered and put down the proud.

touching consolation of this code of morals—the true philosopher would recognize in it the consummation of his highest aspiration after human excellence. And this may still be urged with effect as an incontrovertible evidence of the marvellous excellence of CHRIST's teaching.

To other minds the wonderful adaptation to human wants of the scheme of Redemption—the astonishing mercy of the Atonement, its philosophical suitableness to the otherwise helpless state of sinners, appears to be no product or possible invention of human thought, but on the face of it, a proof of Divine dispensation.

Of course above all these evidences, which are mainly addressed to the intellect, is the testimony of conscience, the intense love and gratitude of him who feels that he is partaker of the inestimable benefits of the Gospel of CHRIST—his sins pardoned and done away, his life and actions guided by the Spirit of Grace, and that he is living in a good hope of happiness eternal. " He that doeth the will of GOD shall know the doctrine, that it is of CHRIST." And, analogously, those who are living in all the ordinances of the Church blameless, guiding their lives in her holy ways, these accept the testimony of the Church as of unquestionable cogency, and require no other evidence for their belief.

Nevertheless it is well for even the holiest and

sincerest Christian to be furnished with arguments
to meet the cavils of the day, if not for their own
sake, yet for the sake of those who might be influenced, and saved from unbelief by their charitable aid, and therefore it appears to me, that
the matter ought to be widely spread through our
popular literature—in order to guard the unwary
against the snares with which their faith is sur-
rounded.

I do not however think it is necessary always to
meet sceptics with serious argument. It seems
to admit that what they say really deserves consideration. Of course, if you think that you may
possibly win them from their error, then, for
charity's sake, you may seriously refute them.
But I mean rather that, for your own sake, it is
quite unnecessary to enter into discussion. Suppose, for instance, an unbeliever says there is no
GOD, you have simply to say that you for your
part believe, or rather are sure there is. To deny
that there is a GOD Who made heaven and earth,
and all that is in them, is in your view as unreasonable as to deny that the shortest way from one
point to another is a straight line, or that the
whole is greater than a part. The fact does not
need discussion, it is self-evident.

Suppose, again, another philosopher tells you
that GOD created a single animalcule or monad,
and that from this animalcule there grow up, in

course of years, all the vast variety of the animal
world—lions, tigers, sparrows, cockchafers, and
all the rest, man included, you have only to say
that you believe no such thing—he can give you
no proof whatever, it is merely his fancy or private
opinion ; you believe that GOD created all these
things when it was most suitable, that is, as the
earth became fitted for their reception. It is
mere waste of time to argue seriously with a man
who puts forward his own mere private opinion
as a scientific fact. Of course it is not meant to
dispute many curious facts brought forward by
Mr. Darwin and his friends about the development of species—the dying out of some, the improvement of others. The pigeon-fancier or the
cattle-breeder can confirm these statements. But
the monstrous theory founded on these few facts
of the evolution of the animal creation, man included, from a single speck or monad—appears
to me the wildest and most unfounded fiction
which was ever devised by the brain of man, and
really not deserving serious refutation. Never
was a more evident myth palmed on human cre-
dibility. A writer in the last *Contemporary Review*
for December tells us that " No one even slightly
acquainted with scientific methods and results
can for a moment brook the idea of any interference with the laws of external nature by prayer
. . . . the physical nexus between phenomena, in

their ceaseless flux and reflux is never broken;
while the order in which the phenomena appear
is governed by the rigour of an adamantine law.
. . . . . This conception of the absolute fixity of
physical law is one which the progress of science
has made axiomatic." That is to say, "Those
are my opinions, and whoever thinks differently,
all I can say is, he is the biggest fool on earth."
Where is the proof of this modern theory? There
is none whatever. It is contrary to the Bible,
contrary to common sense, contrary to history.
We know for certain that GOD has continually
interfered in the course of nature—for aught we
know He may be continually doing so now. What
object could there be in creating this visible universe if He took no further interest about it?
The notion is absurd. It is only a mere clique
of men who fancy themselves philosophers, and
some weak-minded persons who think their dogmas
very fine, who hold these opinions about the non-
interference of GOD in the work of His hands.
All the rest of the world, the vast preponderance
of human intellect believe, and always have believed, that the Great Creator of heaven and earth
is Ruler and Governor of His work.

Take, again, the assertion of Strauss and others
of his stamp, that there never was such a person
as JESUS CHRIST,—that the incidents of His life
are too marvellous to be believed, or that they rest

on no sure foundation of history. Archbishop
Whately has shown in his amusing brochure
"Historic Doubts relative to Napoleon Buonaparte," that you might just as well deny the existence of that eminent personage, as deny the
existence of JESUS CHRIST. Who was Napoleon
Buonaparte according to the accounts we read of
him ? An obscure adventurer from the Island of
Corsica, is said to have placed himself at the
head of the great French nation, and to have exercised despotic authority over the most intellectual people in the world. By the means of
conscription he dragged hundreds of thousands
of them unwillingly from their homes, and made
them fight for his ambitious projects, and endure
all sorts of hardships and privations : thousands
of them being put to violent death. With their
help he invaded and conquered all the nations of
Europe. He occupied successively Berlin, Vienna,
Madrid, Moscow, &c. At last the English beat
him at Waterloo, and sent him to pass the end
of his days on the solitary rock of S. Helena.
Was there ever such a rigmarole or improbable
fiction ? And what authority have we for all
these statements ? Newspapers ! Is it not notorious that newspapers are written merely to be
sold ; and that the editors put into them anything which may tickle the public fancy, and
promote the sale of their publication ? Besides,

suppose newspaper editors to be the most trustworthy of men, how can we be sure that they
themselves were accurately informed ? They did
not see all these wonderful things,—they took
their information second-hand from special correspondents and persons of that sort, whose
business it was to make up a good story to fill
the paper. So it is certainly most probable that
all this story about Napoleon and his exploits
was nothing more than a conspiracy amongst
newspaper writers and stock-jobbers for their
mutual advantage. There may have been some
slight foundation of fact. But all this super-
structure of improbable fiction which interested
persons have built upon it is clearly unworthy of
the credit of a philosophical and inquiring age !
Very like these are the arguments brought forward by modern sceptics, who affect to disbelieve
the history and life of our LORD JESUS CHRIST.

There is another mode of meeting the question
adopted by Lacordaire in his Conferences delivered at Notre Dame some few years ago. His
argument is this,—that no great public event, or
series of events, which have exercised a great influence in the world, could be "foisted into the
web of history," unless they were true. He
gives a supposed instance from French history,
which I forget, and will substitute the following.
—Suppose a person were to publish a book con-

taining a statement of this sort. "In the year 1800 Napoleon Buonaparte gathered a great army of 150,000 men at Boulogne, together with a vast flotilla and fleet of men-of-war, and, having conquered and dispersed the fleet commanded by Nelson, he invaded with his army the shores of Sussex. The English hastily got together all the troops they could collect and fought a great battle at Dorking, in which Napoleon, with his usual good fortune, was triumphant. After this he took possession of London without opposition, deposed King George III. and the Lord Mayor, substituted a French Prefect for the latter, and himself reigned at the palace of St. James' for three years; after which the English rose simultaneously against him, and drove him and his army out of the country." Suppose any person were to publish a statement like this, it is absolutely impossible that it could ever obtain a footing in history,—it would be looked on as a mere joke, and rather a bad one too.

Well, look at the historical account of the life of our LORD JESUS CHRIST,—Who wrought the greatest moral change that was ever effected in the world's history, Whose birth was of that importance that the whole civilised world dates the events of history according as they have happened before or after that great event. We have not only the history of the Divine Person re-

corded by the four Evangelists, but we have also
the evidence of Roman and Jewish historians
bearing testimony to the growing up of the
Christian Church, until more or less gradually
the whole Roman world with its Emperor em-
braced the Christian faith.   Every history of the
world which was ever written admits into its
pages this account of these great events.   They
are, in fact, the basis of modern society.   Such
· is the testimony of history.   And it is clearly an
impossibility that these important events should
have been "foisted into the web of history" if
they were not true.   To say that JESUS CHRIST
never lived would contradict all the principles of
human knowledge.

Or to say that our LORD JESUS CHRIST was a
mythical character, like Hercules or Prometheus,
is absurd—because the time when He appeared
was a civilised age.   Athens was the centre of
philosophy, Rome the head of political power.
The art of writing was universally known.   It is
impossible that any fictitious person could ever
be imagined and believed in, much less exercise
the wide-spread influence which was exercised by
CHRIST.

Distance of time does not at all weaken the
truth of history in the case of notorious persons.
We are as sure there was such a person as Augustus
Cæsar as that there is such a person as Queen

Victoria. No sane person doubts the former. No one who is competent to judge of the truth of history, unless it be for the sake of promoting some cherished prejudice, can doubt of the reality of the life and actions of our LORD JESUS CHRIST.

CHAPTER X.

SCEPTICS, ANCIENT AND MODERN.—GROUNDS OF BELIEF.—
TESTIMONY, INDUCTION, DEDUCTION.—THEIR RESPECTIVE
VALUE.—CREED OF THE SCEPTIC.

THE Sceptics were a sect of ancient philosophers,
whose peculiarity was to doubt everything; and
what is remarkable, they seemed to like it rather
than otherwise, they doubted on principle—and
were rather proud of it. Instead of setting to
work manfully and clearing up their doubts, they
sat down quietly content to know nothing for
certain. They were called "Pyrrhonists" from
their founder, and "Aporetici," because they
were "poor creatures" who could not make up
their minds about anything.

It was natural enough for men of those days
to be doubtful on many important subjects, because they had not received a Revelation from
GOD. Yet they seem to have doubted about some
things which most men would think sufficiently
evident. Some doubted of their own existence, till
one of them propounded the celebrated formula
of Metaphysics, "Cogito, ergo sum" (I think,

therefore I am.) Similar arguments one would have thought might have occurred to them. An Epicurean might have said "Prandeo, ergo sum" (I eat my dinner, therefore I am sure I am alive.) A Stoic might have pinched himself and said, "Sentio, ergo sum," (I feel, therefore I am.) No one could dispute any of these propositions. Another of the ancient philosophers doubted whether there was any such thing as motion; upon which his companion, to prove his error, got up and walked about the room. This is the famous mode of argument called "solvitur ambulando" ("the question is solved by walking,") which applies to matters which can be settled at once, and decided without more ado. I once heard of a sceptic who doubted whether his life was not all a dream, and his dreams his real existence.

We hear of some men who doubt whether there is a GOD. The best answer to this would, I think, come under the formula "solvitur ambulando." Take your sceptical friend out with you for a walk into the fields laden with corn and fruit, show him the glorious landscape, the beautiful flowers and trees, the cattle grazing on the hills; or at night bid him walk with you under the canopy of heaven, and gaze on the stars and silvery moon—quote to him the beautiful words of the Psalmist, "The heavens declare the glory of GOD, and the firmament showeth His handy work. . . . . . O LORD, how glorious are Thy works, in wisdom hast Thou made them all." He must, indeed, be amongst the " Aporetici" if he fail to acknowledge the truth of your appeal. To most men the existence of a GOD, the Maker and Ruler of the Universe, seems as self-evident as their own existence—the denying His existence would seem just as nonsensical as denying that there was such a thing as motion. " Sum, ergo Deus est," (I am, therefore, there is a GOD,) seems to me, I confess, as self-evident an argument as " cogito, ergo sum."

There are other sceptics who, as I said in the last chapter, deny the plainest historical facts; for instance, the birth, death, and resurrection of our Blessed LORD as recorded in the Gospels. It may be well, therefore to analyze the ground of belief. Take first our belief in passing events— contemporary history—for each day which passes is evolving history. What are the grounds of our belief in what is going on in the world? Well, I suppose most of us receive much of the know- ledge we have from the public journals. I get my *Times* every morning, and in half-an-hour or less, if I have time to read it, I know all that is going on in the world, I am master of all the details of contemporary history. I see perhaps that the Queen prorogued Parliament yesterday. But how can I be quite sure of the fact? First,

I know that it was expected that she would do so on that particular day; then I am aware that the *Times* sends reporters to the House of Lords who write down all that occurs. Thirdly, I know that if the *Times* gave false information on the subject, there are scores of other papers which would convict it of incorrectness, and it would forfeit all its prestige, and cease to be relied on as the leading journal. Therefore I have no hesitation in accepting the fact that the Queen really did prorogue Parliament at the time mentioned. Besides the prorogation of Parliament, there are a thousand other facts which may equally be received as true—the police and law reports, sporting intelligence, births, marriages, and deaths. I know that it is the business of the *Times* to collect right information on all these subjects, that it has every possible facility for so doing, that it would be ruin to it commercially if it failed; therefore I receive the intelligence contained in it without hesitation. Not, indeed, in all respects. I do not take for granted all that is contained in the leading articles for instance, for that consists not so much of facts as of opinions; and these I take the liberty of forming for myself. The letters of special correspondents, written in haste from distant countries, in the midst of war and tumult, may not be quite accurate. Telegraphic despatches often "require confirmation;" statements made by

I

strong partizans cannot always be implicitly relied
on.   Still, looking at the mass of general information contained in a sheet of the *Times*, we
may take it as an accurate picture of the history
of the day, which may be regarded as substantial
truth.

It is possible that the editor may sometimes be
hoaxed, or it is conceivable, at least, on sceptical
principles, that he may choose to play off a hoax
himself.   The authorities in Printing House
Square might publish a sort of sham paper for the
fun of it—set down a number of marriages between people who never thought of such a thing,
an account of doings in all parts of the world
which never took place—sham law reports, and
fictitious debates in Parliament—" Mysterious disappearance of the Archbishop of Canterbury,"
" Revolution in Russia," "Remarkable Longevity,"
" Financial Panic,"—it is, I say, physically possible, but so utterly incredible that it would not
enter into any one's calculation, except indeed, of
the sceptic.   The same argument which applies to
contemporary history is applicable also to the
history of the past.   It is possible physically that
our standard histories, on which we rely, may all
be wrong.   Clarendon's History of the Rebellion
may, sceptically speaking, be a myth, and no such
persons may have lived as Charles I. and Oliver
Cromwell, but speaking according to common

sense, the idea is simply ridiculous. On sceptical principles, Cæsar's Commentaries, Tacitus, Suetonius, may be all fabrications ; no such persons as Julius Cæsar, Augustus, or Tiberius, may have existed: but any one who should avow such sceptical notions would be judged to be talking nonsense. So in respect to the Life and Death of our LORD JESUS CHRIST, recorded as they are by four Evangelists,—the idea of His history being a fable, is absurd. In the latter case the testimony is stronger than in any other. We do not hear that Tacitus, or any Roman or Greek historian, or Clarendon in more recent times, submitted to death in testimony of the truth of his history, but almost all of the first Evangelists and preachers of the Gospel sealed their testimony by their blood. We judge, therefore, without doubt that their testimony is the truth. Even as mere human testimony we should be constrained to accept the history of the life and actions of our LORD JESUS CHRIST. But we believe that the account written in the Gospel is further attested by Divine authority. On this, however, I will not now dilate.

Besides the certainty which we obtain from undoubted testimony, there are other certain and unquestionable evidences, on the strength of which we firmly believe things. The most reliable, perhaps, is induction. Induction is the foundation of almost all science. For instance, we throw

a stone up into the air, and observe that it always
comes down again, if we throw it up a hundred
times.   We have no doubt that if other persons
threw up stones on the other side of the world, or
if they threw up other things, they would be sure
to come down again.   It is one of those "laws"
which GOD has given to the universe, and is
evident to our common experience.   We have,
therefore, a sure induction, involving a principle
—namely, the principle of gravitation, which is
found to apply to all parts of the world, and to
explain a vast variety of scientific facts.

But there are a great many things equally undoubted, which, nevertheless, we cannot ascertain
of our own knowledge, but with regard to which
it would be absurd to be sceptical.   We can accept the facts on testimony.   For instance, philosophers tell us that water boils at a certain
temperature at the top of mountains.   Well,
some of us, perhaps, have not been at the top of
mountains, and if we had been, did not happen
to take a tea-kettle with us.   Nevertheless, all
scientific men tell us that it certainly is the case,
and we see no reason to disbelieve them.   This
sort of knowledge embraces a large portion of the
knowledge which we accept as trustworthy, and
add to our intellectual store.   It is made up of
testimony and induction united.   To unscientific
persons who cannot make experiments for them-

selves, almost all philosophic knowledge rests on
this foundation.

But besides testimony and induction, which
when formally perfect we may implicitly rely on,
there is also the argument of deduction, by which
we infer truth from ascertained premisses. And
this sort of argument may be divided into mathematical demonstration, and moral, or philosophical
deduction. Mathematical demonstration, such as
Euclid's Elements, and a vast variety of calculations in geometry and arithmetic, may be implicitly trusted; but moral deduction is not so
certain, because it rests more on human reason
than on actual facts. "Nothing," says Sir Hum-
phrey Davy, "is more difficult, and requires more
caution than philosophical deduction." There
are many very true deductions, but others which
are not reliable. We know that it is possible for
philosophers to be run away with by their imagination. Old people will sometimes tell the same
old story over and over again till they quite believe it. So philosophers will dwell so long on
some very doubtful deduction that they come to
have no question in their own minds that it is
true. A vast variety of notions and theories of
this sort issue continually from the press, which
may or may not be true: certainly they are not
to be accepted with the same confidence as we
accept what is presented to us by testimony or

induction. Master minds indeed like Newton's, who have not only powerful insight, but also judgment and discrimination, may deduce theories which the intellectual world would accept eventually with the assurance of perfect conviction. But men of inferior calibre rush into conclusions with undue precipitancy. They may or may not be correct.· For instance, a geologist has observed with great care the phenomena of the earth's surface, and specially of the British Isles, and he tells me that there was a time when the country which we inhabit was submerged in the ocean, or covered with perpetual snow. This is rather startling, if I have never thought of the matter. I do not deny the fact, but I ask for further proof of his assertion. The geologist is so good as to explain to me his reason, and I acquiesce at least in the probability of his theory. Another geologist tells us that there was a time when the British Channel and the German Ocean where all dry land —that England was united with the Continent— and " the Thames was a tributary of the Rhine." I listen to his reasons, but they do not quite satisfy me. I do not quite see it. His arguments do not seem to me sufficient to warrant the hypothesis. Another man goes further, and tells me that he has been thinking over the matter all his life, and has come to the conclusion, as his father did before him, that man was not originally created in the image of God, but that he was derived by evolution from an ape. I ask him for his proof, but he has very little or none to give, only a very fixed and decided opinion of his own. I see plainly that, clever, and able, and earnest as he may be, he has taken up a notion which is not tenable, and dwelt on it and told the same story over and over again, until he has convinced himself of its truth. I can only regret that he should have bestowed his time and acknowledged talents on such unprofitable labour.

From what is said above, it will be seen that our sure ground of belief as to ordinary facts of history or daily life is testimony—our best ground for scientific facts is induction—but that deduction or argument from these facts must needs partake of the uncertainty inseparable from the action of the human mind. It depends not on facts, but on man's uncertain reasoning.

P.S.—Pascal has somewhere in his works, "The Creed or No-Creed of a Sceptic." The following is an adaptation of the idea to the present times:

"I am not sure whether I believe in God the Father Almighty, Maker of heaven and earth. To call God our Father is anthropomorphism, and therefore I suppose not philosophic. God may have made the materials of the world in the shape of nebulæ or star dust; but I am not certain.

"I do not know whether or no I have a spirit or soul within me, or whether my thoughts do not proceed from some collocation of the molecules of the brain.

"Whence I came I am entirely ignorant, whether GOD created the first father of our race in His own image, or whether we are not all descended from some 'hairy quadruped' or ape.

"I have no notion why I was placed in the world, or what I have to do now I am here. If a good GOD placed me here I suppose I ought to worship Him and try to know what He would have me do. But if I was evolved by some law or order of Nature, I cannot make that the object of worship.

"As I know not whence I came, so I know not whither I go, whether at death I shall fall into a state of annihilation, whether I shall be reduced to my original atoms and absorbed into the general order of nature, or whether I shall have to give an account of the deeds done in the flesh, and have my portion accordingly, in heaven or hell.

"If I have to give account for my actions I fear it will go hard with me, for I have done many evil things, and I have no ground on which I can hope for remission of sins.

"Behold then my wretched condition. Yet I

suppose I shall live and die in it; for though I am in doubt about all these things, it is not my intention to try and find them out. It is too much trouble to have to make up one's mind about such things. I suppose I shall glide smoothly along the stream of life. I shall eat and drink, and to-morrow die. Then perhaps I shall know about these things—perhaps not. But may it not then be too late? I am sure I cannot tell."

CHAPTER XI.

At a recent meeting of the British Association,
Professor Tyndall gave an interesting lecture on
the "Use of the Imagination in Science." I
only remember one of his illustrations which was
to the effect that the tail of a comet was some
fifty thousand miles in length, but so extremely
subtile that it might be all packed into a lady's
portmanteau. I think he added, "if it were
packed close enough." Whether this was a sly
hit at some of his lady friends who travel, as
some ladies will, with unusually large portmanteaus I cannot say, but certainly the illustration
showed a lively imagination in the lecturer.

At another meeting of the same august body
Sir William Thompson, the President, ventured a
good way into the region of imagination. It is,
as we all know, a favourite dogma of modern
philosophers that all the organised varieties of
animal and vegetable life have been evolved out

of a single germ or monad; but the question is,
how did the primordial monad come into exist-
ance,—at least on this planet? Sir W. Thompson's conjecture is this—that when the earth
was cooling down from its incandescent state and
beginning to be crusted over with solid matter, a
stone or fragment from some broken planet which
was floating above in the region of space,—one
of those aerolites which are seen in the shape of
the November meteors, retaining fortunately a
seed of ancient moss or lichen, conveyed the
necessary germ to the barren earth, and from that
beginning grew up the fauna and flora of our
present globe,—the corn which forms the staple
of our food, the stately oak and cedar of the
forest, the vast variety of the animal race from
man down to the smallest animalcule, all sprang
in the course of ages from this primordial
monad.

Mr. Darwin in his publications exemplifies,
perhaps, more than any one, the use of the imagination in science,—in truth, the whole of his
system is simply imaginative. Some writers on
analogous subjects show a considerable defect in
this valuable quality. One principal objection
which Dr. Colenso finds to the account of the
Deluge is that he cannot imagine how the snipes
and vultures were fed and kept alive.

As the use of imagination is recommended by

such high authority, I will venture to try my
hand at the explanation of certain phenomena
which a few years ago not a little puzzled the
philosophers, and, I believe, have never yet been
satisfactorily accounted for; I mean the discovery
of a large quantity of a rude kind of flint-weapons in the valley of the Somme near Amiens.
The papers were for some weeks full of the question. I venture, not without diffidence, to lay
the fruits of my own imagination before my
readers.

My notion is that the remarkable accumulation
of flint weapons in that particular spot is referable
to the gorilla period, or rather the transition
period between the gorilla and man. We know,
so at least Mr. Darwin tells us, that the last
development of the animal race before the appearance of man was "a hairy quadruped furnished with tail and pointed ears, probably
arboreal in his habits." Now the problem to be
solved is, how did creatures of this sort become
developed into man? I wonder it has not struck
our imaginative philosopher that it must certainly
have been by the discovery of the use of flints.
In the early age of the world the use of flints
must have made almost as great a difference in
the manners and customs of gorillas as the art of
printing, or the discovery of steam has brought
about in more modern times. Consider well the

facts. These creatures of arboreal habits dwelt chiefly in the trees, clinging to the branches with their tails,—fed probably on acorns and beech nuts, when by one of those fortunate occurrences, which sometimes happen, such as the falling of the apple which suggested to Newton the theory of gravitation, or the boiling over of a tea-kettle which was the means of the discovery of the power of steam, the use of a sharp-edged flint may have arisen in this way. It is remarkable, as Pope says in his Rape of the Lock,—

" What great events from trivial causes spring."

Perhaps some gorilla cut his finger with a flint, or more probably his toe, for being "arboreal in his habits" he would naturally not be clever in treading on the ground. Being of a philosophical and imaginative tone of mind it would occur to him that if the flint was sharp enough to cut his finger or his foot, it might be used for cutting other things. I do not suppose that any patents were taken out in those days, else the discoverer of the use of the flint might certainly have made a fortune. The probability is, that when once discovered, the use of flint came into very general use. And imagine only the radical change which this one discovery must have made. Instead of living on acorns and beech-nuts as heretofore, and having no better shelter in bad weather than

a few broken boughs put together in the shape of
an umbrella,—such as the apes of a low degree
of civilization even now use in the forests of
Africa,—the gorilla, with the use of his flint-axe
could cut down trees and build a hut,—he could
dig roots for his subsistence,—the truffle, the
pig-nut, or even the potato; then he could defend himself against the larger animals, and kill
the smaller for his use; he could open oysters
and split cocoa-nuts. He could pare his nails,
nay, perhaps, shave himself! What a range of
new thought and potential culture would be
open before him!

It is probable that at this critical period of the
world's history, as at many other critical periods,
there arose a gorilla who was above the age in
which he lived, a pioneer to lead society onward
in the march of intellect. We can well imagine
that some such gorilla arose—a Confucius, or a
Solon amongst them. Let us suppose a gorilla
of this advanced intellect summoning his fellows
to a conference on the banks of the Somme,—as
a gathering of the British Association might be
held at Brighton. " My good friends and fellow-
gorillas," we can imagine him saying, "we are
assembled together at a great crisis of our history.
By the law of order we have been steadily advancing onwards, and have now made not a step only,
but a great stride in civilization. I need not

MAY HAVE USED THE FLINTS.   127

point out to you the immense advantage of the
power of flint. It is an era in the world's history. From being arboreal in our habits, we
have come to walk firmly on the ground, and to
carry our heads erect."

[The advanced gorilla evidently anticipated the
splendid idea contained in the lines of Ovid :—

> " Pronaque cum spectent animalia cætera terram,
> Os homini sublime dedit, cœlumque tueri
> Jussit, et erectos ad sidera tollere vultus."[1]]

"But, gentlemen,—I mean gorillas,—there is
still one great drawback to our progress—one
circumstance which mars our aspirations. I need
scarcely mention that I allude to our tails.
Formerly when we were arboreal in our habits,
the caudal appendage was valuable and useful.
It aided us greatly in our arboreal climbings.
But now that we aspire to walk with form erect,
and raise our eyes to heaven, it is evident that
our tails are greatly in our way. Besides they
are often very uncomfortable when one sits down
to dinner—as, of course, all well-bred gorillas do
(hear, hear). They are, in fact, a sad incum-
brance. And just at this critical time the great
order of nature has furnished us, in the discovery

[1] While others of GOD's creatures downward look
Towards earth, He gave to man a face sublime,
And bade him gaze on heaven, and contemplate
The starry sphere with countenance erect.

of flint, with the means of disencumbering ourselves of our tails, which I must say are neither
useful nor ornamental."

Great applause followed the termination of the
wise gorilla's speech. A general enthusiasm was
kindled, and it required but a little more encouragement to induce the assembly to fall to
work, with but few dissentient voices, and cut
off each other's tails with the flint weapons, and
having done so, to fling their knives, tails and
all, into the river. The tails floated down to
the "melancholy ocean," the flint-weapons were
imbedded in the Somme, for the benefit of future
philosophers. And in commemoration of this
great event, it was enacted that when each young
gorilla which was born had its tail cut off, the
flint-weapon was considered sacred, and flung
into the nearest river; which is the only way of
accounting for the numerous weapons of that sort
which are from time to time discovered. Of
course, after a few generations had had their tails
cut off, they gradually dwindled into a mere
stump, which we now call the *os coccygis*.

Now I challenge any one of my readers to
show that there is any flaw in this argument,
I mean on the principle of the use of the imagination in science, advocated by Professor Tyndall.
Mr. Darwin says that no explanation has " ever
been given of the loss of the tail by certain apes

and men." Well, I have given one. There is the fact which forms the fundamental basis of the modern theory,—the development of man from the arboreal animal, and next the fact of the more or less sudden disappearance of the tail about the time when flint weapons were invented. Surely it requires little more than to put two and two together, and we have the whole history before us, and a very important part of history it is. In fact, if one considers well, even without the use of the imagination, it must have been the most critical period of the world. Nothing perhaps in the history of man can be conceived more important than the era of his development from the brute. Then, in confirmation of the above theory, we have the traditional apologue of the "Fox who had lost his tail." How easy after such a lapse of time to mistake the gorilla for the fox. One might also "imagine" that the old song which was made when Lord Collingwood nearly caused a mutiny by cutting off his sailors' pig-tails, bears somehow on the subject,—

> " We didn't mind it now and then
>   A leg or arm to spare, sir,
> But all our tails to lose at once,
>   'Twas cutting work to bear, sir."

It must be manifest how much preferable is the use of the imagination, recommended by Professor Tyndall, to the old-fashioned method of

philosophical analysis. "The old Baconian induction was," as Canon Rawlinson said at the
Church Congress, "a careful interrogation of
nature, and its legitimate object was to establish
as absolutely true such general laws as could
be distinctly proved by an examination of all
the phenomena. Modern science has substituted
for the laborious investigation of facts the easy
method of hypothesis. The authors of these
beautiful systems, which they have spun out of
their own imagination, naturally become ena-
moured of them." Of course they do. I can
assure you I feel very proud of the bantling which
my own imagination has created. It seems to
me just as promising as any of Professor Tyndall's
or Mr. Darwin's either.

CHAPTER XII.

MUCH is said and written in the present day
about the origin and first cause of things—whence
life and motion proceed?—what are the first processes of the operations of nature? Many things
of which we had hitherto known only the existence are traced up to their cause: at least, many
clever guesses are made, and sometimes ingenious
proofs are not wanting. The forces of nature—
light, heat, electricity, motion, are more or less
investigated and, to a certain extent, explained.
And yet with all the scientific analysis there is
always something beyond the power of human
discovery—something which science cannot trace
or prove, but is obliged to accept by faith, or by
common sense.

Let me give one or two examples. Suppose I
raise my arm, what is the power by which I do
so? We know that it is by the power of the
muscles—the power which they have to contract,

and so act by the leverage of the sinews on the
bones.   But what causes the muscles to contract
so as to raise the arm ?   It is the operation of the
nerves which act upon the muscles.   But how
are the nerves thus set in motion ?   It is by the
impulse of the brain, of which they are, as it were,
expansions or feelers.   Thus the brain operates
on the nerves, the nerves on the muscles, and the
muscles raise the arm.

All this is easily ascertainable.   But then there
is another step which is not so readily explained,
at least, not by natural science.   What is it that
causes the brain to act, and to put forth this
energy?   What is it that really sets in motion
those various organs, the operation of which we
have so far traced ?   *It is the Will*—the will of
man—impalpable, undiscernible by scientific analysis, yet operating everywhere throughout the
world—everywhere at least where man is found.

And what a wonderful force is the will of man !
For if, as we have seen, it is the will of man by
which the arm is raised, then everything which
the united immaterial and material power of man
accomplishes is traceable to the same energy.
What wonders throughout the world has the will
of man accomplished, what cities has it built,
what ships has it constructed, what vast extent of
territory has it cultivated, what works of art, of
literature, has it wrought!   All these things has

the will of man accomplished through those organs which God has provided for his use. All the works which man has wrought have proceeded from that impalpable immaterial essence or agency, or impulse, which we call the Will.

These thoughts, however, are but preliminary to the much wider inquiry into the origin of the will of man itself, and, in fact, into the origin of the visible and invisible universe with all its complicated arrangements and forces. The works of man, great and important as they are when considered by themselves, yet are but inconsiderable when compared with the vast universe, with all the wonderful operations which it exhibits.

A philosopher once received a visit from a friend who unhappily was an atheist. The philosopher had lately purchased a beautiful globe, which caught the eye of the visitor. " Who made you that beautiful globe ?" said the atheist. " Who made it ?" said the philosopher, " why no one—it made itself !" The atheist perceived at once the satire conveyed in his friend's observation, and we may hope profited by it.

Strange it is that there should be men in the nineteenth century who have gone back to the darkness of heathen ages, and actually believe that this world, and all that is in it, and all the wonderful processes of nature, should have come into existence, and should go on in their course without the intervention of an all-wise and all-governing Will.

Let us endeavour, by the help of modern science, to trace up some of the operations of nature to their source. Consider the simplest, or at least the commonest, of all things—the bread which we daily eat. Whence comes it? We know that it is made of flour ground in the mill, and baked in the oven, and that the flour is made of the grain which grows in our fields. But how is it that the grain grows in the fields? It is sown by the labourer. But how is it that when sown in the field the grain germinates and puts forth first the tender blade, then the stalk, and then the ear, filled with food? The grain which is sown dry and hard, is caused to germinate by the operation of the rain and heat, and thereby its chemical properties are called forth into action, and " a definite molecular action is the result." But how is it that the rain falls in due season? The rain falls from the clouds; and the clouds, how are they spread over the land? The clouds are formed by the condensation of the invisible vapour of water, which is contained in the air. And whence the constant supply of this vapour? It is drawn up from the sea and moistened surface of the earth. It falls upon the land, and is drained off by the rivers and watercourses; and again and again taken up and distributed as

before to fertilize the earth. We might go on to
many other steps in the process. What causes
the rarefaction and condensation by which the
water is drawn up into the air, collected into
clouds, and descends in drops upon the earth?
It is caused by the concurrence of warmer and
colder strata of air. The air is rarefied and drawn
up mainly at the tropics, and the consequent
rushing in of colder currents to supply the place,
results in the formation of those wholesome winds,
the soft and temperate breezes from the south, the
strong west winds, or the cold currents from the
east and north, whereby the stagnation of the
atmosphere is prevented, and the operations of
nature are continued from year to year, and the
earth yields its increase for the wants of man. We
might go on from one fact to another, the theory
of heat and electricity, the influence of the sun
and other agencies. But after all we come to the
question, Who or What caused all the wonderful
dependence of the forces of nature one upon another? And the answer at which we arrive is
that it is the *Will of God*. The construction of
this wonderful earth which we inhabit, and all the
elaborate contrivances for the sustentation of its inhabitants, was no fortuitous concurrence of atoms,
coming together of their own accord, any more
than the globe in the philosopher's study was a
fortuitous concurrence of atoms—no mere chance

collocation of molecules, but a determination of mind, an operation of the Creative Will of GOD. That was the real and efficient cause of the universe which we see around us, and of the laws by which creation is governed.

Thus does philosophical analysis, even independently of revelation, prove to us that the primary agent of all existing things, is an Omnipotent Will—the Will of GOD by Whom and through Whom all things were made and continue to exist.

We see, then, that there are two Wills in the world—the Will of GOD and the Will of Man. And here we may discern one reason of the absolute necessity of a constant regulative power in the Will of GOD. The sceptic may say, Why did not GOD make a world in which all should be good and perfect—no power of resistance to His Will? It seems to be an obvious and sufficient answer to the cavil, that GOD created free agents as being of a higher order of beings than creatures without a power of choice. But the existence of beings having a will of their own, absolutely necessitates the constant interference of the higher Will, to set right the disarrangements caused by the will of the inferior beings. And herein is the highest and most wonderful attribute of GOD's perfection—namely, the power to govern and regulate the perverse wills of beings who are still

not the less free. Hence we see also the strange
misconception of those who could for a moment
imagine that the Will of GOD was "vengeful,
arbitrary, variable, capricious." It is no more
vengeful and capricious than the will of the Judge
who, according to their respective deserts, con-
demns one man to ten years' penal servitude, another to five, and acquits a third. The Will of
GOD is perfect justice, rendering to every man
according to his work.

It would have been a mighty manifestation of
Almighty power and wisdom to have made this
great material universe—the sun, the moon, and
stars, all maintaining their appointed order without power of deviation in the slightest degree—
still greater is the wonder of the animal race, each
in its kind provided with organs for the sustentation and prolongation of its kind. But the
marvel of the universe is man created "in the
image of GOD"—man endowed with will and free-
dom of action—free to choose the course which
he will take. To govern the order of the human
race—their relations with each other, their national
combinations, their wonderful powers of varied
action—to combine all this in one harmonious
whole, to regulate continually the destinies of
free agents, this it is which fills us with highest
awe and admiration.

But this is the province of religion, not of

science. Mark the wide difference in the power of each. Science can investigate and discover, to a certain extent, the mysteries of the material world, the strong forces of nature, the relations of organic or inorganic matter, but it is utterly powerless to appreciate the Will or moral nature of man, it can conceive only a fixed order of nature, things growing up, and going on according to some definite unbending law. But of the relation of the Will of GOD to man, the moral choice, the power of prayer, the graces of the Spirit, it has not the most remote conception. All this is the province of religion.

I hope I may be pardoned for adding to my imperfect remarks the following admirable passage from a Paper in *Fraser's Magazine*, for September, 1873, by Leonard Woolsey Bacon, Clerk :—

"It may be freely granted that according to the view here presented the universe is incalculably, inconceivably complicated. Professor Tyndall's universe is a neat machine, having its object, if not its cause, in itself. If it was made for a toy to see how smoothly it would spin, and how aptly part would play upon part, and mechanical, chemical and vital systems would work together, it is altogether successful. . . . But if the Christian idea of prayer and all that it implies is to be admitted, if we are to believe that this prodigious machine of the physical system is geared to run in connection and subordination with a moral and spiritual system, which is further complicated, wheel within wheel, by the presence of a thousand millions of independent wills; in such sort that all the tricks, turns, and changes of the material system shall coincide precisely with the exigency of the whole moral system, and of its every individual member, bringing to prayer its timely answer, to pride and folly its fit discipline, to sin its fatherly chastisement, to the Church deliverance and triumphs, to mankind at last complete Salvation,—if such be the condition of the universe, the mind grows bewildered in the attempt to conceive it. The truth is that science in its eagerness to grasp the material object of the universe altogether ignores the reason of the world's being, namely, the training to perfection of the wills of men."

Since writing the above, I have seen the report of the meeting of the British Association for Science, and have copied from it the following remarks of the President of the department of Biology, Professor Allman.

" He did not wish to shut his eyes to the difficulties in the way of accepting the theory of Evolution when carried to the extreme length for which some of its advocates contend . . . . .

Even accepting as a great truth the theory of
Evolution he would not attribute to it more than
it could fairly claim, for there remains a residual
phenomenon still unaccounted for.   No physical
hypothesis founded on any indisputable fact has
yet explained the origin of this primordial proto-
plasm, and above all, of its marvellous properties
which render evolution possible, in heredity and
adaptivity, for these properties are the cause and
not the effect of evolution.   For the cause of this
cause we have sought in vain amongst the physical forces which surround us, until we are at
last compelled to rest upon *an independent volition*
—a far-seeing intelligent design."   It is something to have recognized by physicists the great
truth of an independent volition, or personal
Deity in the work of creation.   But surely this
admission involves at least the possibility of a
continually acting volition, i.e., a divine Providence in the affairs of the world.   In reading the
report of the discussion at this meeting I was
much gratified by observing the tone of modera-
tion, and the general absence of the declaration
of atheistic opinion; which I trust may be taken
as a guarantee that the recent attacks on religion
are to be attributed to a few only amongst the
philosophers of the age, and not to be considered
as the tone of feeling of the general body of men
of science.

In the same spirit Mr. Powell, M.P., proposed
a vote of thanks to the lecturer on Molecules.
"He was thankful for the manly manner in
which Professor Maxwell had acknowledged the
existence of a Great Primary Cause. As long as
the scientific world acknowledged and proclaimed
the existence of a final (?) cause, and religion and
science joined hand in hand together, both might
safely advance from triumph to triumph without
halting or doubting."

CHAPTER XIII.

IT is a very strange and unaccountable fancy which has got into the heads of some of our modern philosophers,—a notion contrary to the belief of all civilized nations, nay rather of all who have lived upon the world since its creation, except it may be some sect of Pagan philosophers, namely, that there is no overruling Providence which governs the affairs of the world, but that all things go on by a certain fixed and unalterable law.

Now, in the first place, though the word "law" may be used popularly to express what they mean by it, strictly and philosophically speaking it is incorrect to use the same term in respect to free agents and inanimate objects. A righteous man obeys the law of GOD by his own free will. The sun and moon obey because they cannot help it. In fact, to use the word "obey" is incorrect. More strictly speaking, man obeys the law, the sun and moon continue in their appointed course. But modern philosophers do not seem to see the distinction.

Again, one would think that not only logical argument, but even common sense would teach people that it was absolutely impossible to prove that there were no deviations from what they term the law of Nature—no supernatural occurrence. In such a case it is altogether impracticable to prove a negative. The affirmative is proved by the universal consent of history that many supernatural occurrences have taken place in the world. But the absolute impossibility of disproving this our philosophers do not seem to understand or choose to ignore; and by the vehemence of their assertion they seem to think to make up for the absence of argument.

."The habitual recognition of law," says Mr. Herbert Spencer, "distinguishes modern thought from ancient thought." "The entire range of inductive philosophy," says Mr. Baden Powell, "is at once based upon, and in every instance tends to confirm, by immense accumulation of evidence the grand truth of the universal order and constancy of natural causes as a primary law of belief." But it would be a mistake to suppose that this our own generation, or even the present century could claim the honour of this grand

discovery. "The apostate Jew Spinoza," says
Bishop Van Mildert in his Boyle Lectures, (Vol.
I., p. 335,) "with extraordinary endowments of
mind, laboured to subvert the principles of the
Gospel. . . . The evident design of his works is to
deny the Creator of the universe. . . . He syste-
matically confounds Him with the material universe, and ascribes to Him no agency but that of an
involuntary or physical energy; making all things
to be derived from Him, not as of His own good
will and pleasure, or as *Creator* of the world, but
by *necessary* emanation from Him as the passive
fountain of existence. He inveighs against those
who deem it necessary to acknowledge any *Creator*
of the world. As the natural consequence of
these Pantheistic, or rather atheistic principles,
he denies a Providence, scoffs at the doctrine of
heaven and hell, and of evil spirits, represents all
divine worship as nugatory, and ridicules as vain
superstition the expectation of rewards and punishments in a future state." Our modern philosophers it will be seen cannot boast of even
originality in their peculiar theories.

Scarcely a doctrine or notion from the cavil of
Colenso to the ape-theory of Darwin has not
been anticipated generations ago, and hence appears the fallacy of the assertion that these ob-
jections to religion are the result of the great
advancement of science in the present generation.

In fact they sprang up when science was comparatively in its infancy.

Bishop Van Mildert, after summing up the labours of the sceptics and infidels of the last century, says, "It is difficult to calculate the mischief effected by these infatuated men. But when we find that to be tainted with infidelity was considered as an almost certain criterion of wit, knowledge, and good breeding, we cannot but suppose that among the vain and superficial, (who constitute always a majority of mankind,) great numbers have been led astray. It is also evident to those who carefully examine their respective labours, that infidels of more recent date have greatly availed themselves of the productions of their predecessors in impiety, so that although for the most part the authors themselves are now unheeded and forgotten, yet through the medium of modern plagiarists they are restored as it were to new life and vigour; though dead, they yet utter the voice of blasphemy, and retain the power of spreading it far and wide."[1]

The good bishop might have been describing the state of things in the present day, except that in spite of the intellectual labours of the Duke of Somerset and Professor Huxley, it cannot quite be said that infidelity is a " criterion of wit,

[1] See Boyle Lectures, Vol. I., p. 367.

knowledge, and good breeding" in the present day. And unlike the Church in past days, the present Church has, we trust, enough of zeal and intellect to repel the aggressions of the enemy.

But to return to our more immediate subject.

The law which these philosophers speak of is as Canon Birks has well described it, "a law with no lawgiver to impose it, no sanction for its observance, no power of choice in its subjects, no consciousness that it is observed, no possibility of being transgressed . . . . the most subtle and evanescent of metaphysical abstractions, if not the most misleading and delusive of terms."[1]

It is contrary to all analogy and reason to suppose a law enacted without any power to carry it out or to enforce it. We know that if human laws were so left to themselves they would be a dead letter. If there were no magistrates or policemen the laws would be nugatory. Law is nothing, of no force, of no avail, unless there be an executive to enforce it. It is altogether un-philosophical and absurd to speak of a law of nature which shall go on of itself. Our unas-sisted reason clearly teaches us that GOD is every-where present guiding and controlling the great universe which He has made, carrying out the laws what He has enacted, upholding and pre-serving the work of His hand.

[1] See the Scripture Doctrine of Creation, p. 154.

GOD has indeed established a law which shall not be broken, and upholds it by His continual Providence—a general law so uniform and consistent that science may consider it as absolute. All calculations and speculations may be founded on the hypothesis that GOD's Almighty power is engaged in carrying out the laws of the universe in so exact and uniform a manner that whatever deviation there may be from them need not in the least interfere with their scientific researches. And yet, at the same time, it is equally true that GOD, without interfering with the ordinary course of nature as a general rule, but maintaining it by His power, does nevertheless, according to His good will and pleasure work miracles, more or less frequent, for special purposes, which, without deranging the course of the world in any perceptible degree, nevertheless suffice not only to show that He is the Ruler and Governor of the universe, but that for special objects He can when He chooses change the law which He has constituted.

And the cause of this occasional variation is obvious. We have seen in the last chapter that there are two wills—the will of GOD, which is absolute, and the will of man, which is subordinate. We all know instinctively that we have a will of our own. There can be no need to go about to prove it, because it is as self-evident as that we exist. It is equally self-evident that

man's will is oftentimes perverse, and contrary to
the Will of GOD, so that GOD changes His purpose
in order to remedy the evil. When GOD first
created man He placed him in the garden of Eden,
in an abode of happiness; but when man rebelled
against His law He drove him forth, and caused
the thorn and the thistle to grow up. At another
time GOD in His just anger destroyed one whole
generation of men by the waters of a Flood.
This change of purpose is often avowed. " I
said indeed," said He to Eli, " that thy house and
the house of thy father, should walk before Me
for ever. But now, the LORD saith, be it far
from Me, for those that honour Me I will honour,
and they that despise Me shall be lightly es-
teemed." Our duty through life—our trial for
eternity, is to conform our will to the Holy Will
of GOD. If we did so, all things might go on in
one regular course. But when man sets himself
against the Will of GOD there is need of the
exertion of GOD's Omnipotent power to control
and rectify the anomaly. It is not that GOD is
inconsistent, but simply just, in His government
of the world.

Another influence which acts upon the Will of
GOD, and induces Him to modify His laws, is the
love and obedience of His creatures. As the
perverseness of their will may cause GOD to act
with severity—to send the storm and tempest, the

pestilence and the drought—so the humble and
faithful prayers of His people induce GOD to with-
draw those chastisements—to send the refreshing
rain and sunshine, to stay the pestilence, or in a
thousand ways to listen with kind condescension
to the request of His people, whom He has invited,
nay commanded, to call on Him.   It is impossible
to know always what are the regular operations
of the law which GOD has constituted and upholds, and what are deviations from the regular
order, which GOD has caused, whether it be to
curb the anomalies of man's perverse will, or to
meet his dutiful prayers.   Ordinarily speaking,
the world goes on by a law, or more properly
speaking, a constituted order, which cannot be
broken.   The philosopher may calculate the revolution of the planets, the eclipse of the sun and
moon.   Very rarely, indeed, some deviation would
be perceptible.   An astronomer watching the
heavens from the towers of Babylon some three
thousand years and more ago may have been perplexed by the unusual prolongation of daylight—
he would be puzzled to account for it, as a modern
philosopher might be puzzled to account for the
appearance of an unexpected comet or meteor—
but nothing further would come of it.   With the
exception of the prolonged daylight all would go
on as before—the next day would be no longer
than other days ; he would note, perhaps, the

singular occurrence in his tablet; and centuries
after, when the Jews brought with them their
Holy Scriptures to Babylon, it would be discovered
that the strange occurrence which had been recorded by some former astronomer was the famous
incident in their history when the sun stood still
upon Gibeon and the moon in the valley of Aja-
lon. Time rolls on, and another notable phenomenon astonishes the wise men of the East. An
unknown star appears in the heavens, and by a
strange impulse they are led to follow it, and it
conducts them to the stable where the infant
SAVIOUR, the SON of GOD, is laid.

With the single exception of the Flood, I do
not think that there is any miracle which could
perceptibly disturb the ordinary laws of nature—
except for the briefest time. And it· is remarkable, though not to be wondered at, that almost
every nation of the earth has preserved the memory
of that event. Very recently a new record of the
Deluge has been discovered among the ruins of
ancient Assyria. This great miracle stands almost
alone with respect to the world-wide impression
which it caused. The wonderful cures wrought
by our LORD during His ministry—the " mighty
works" whereby He demonstrated His divine
power and goodness may, no doubt, have had a
perceptible influence on the " bills of mortality,"
if any such were kept in Judæa in those days—

but no disarrangement could have been made, except momentarily, in the ordinary course of the world.

Therefore, I do not see why philosophers are so jealous of these historical incidents, and so anxious to vindicate the "law" of nature. Their calculations and experiments may proceed without hindrance. The Almighty Ruler carries on His government of the world by the laws which He has given, and when for special purposes He deviates from them, no derangement is caused in the general course of His Providence. The planets roll on in their courses—the forces of nature continue to operate as heretofore. Why, then, should philosophers make all this pother?

To speak the truth, I fear it is simply that an evil spirit of unbelief has perverted their minds, the pride of human intellect has been deceived by the power of evil. It is but one instance amongst a thousand of the perverseness with which evil works in opposition to the Will of God. The heart of man, unsanctified by the spirit of grace, is deceitful and desperately wicked. Sometimes it is led astray by the lusts of the flesh, sometimes by the lust of power. What fearful evils do men of highest intellect work in this world by the sinful desire of lording it over their fellows. At another time Satan works by the pride of intellect. In all ages—not less at the beginning of the

Gospel than in the present day—"philosophy
falsely so-called" has led men away from the
Truth of God.   And in this department of human
evil there is one fearful phenomenon—that men
are not content themselves to depart from the
truth and deny the God who made them, but
with perverse maliciousness they are for ever
striving to drag down others into the same abyss
of misery.   It is one of the most fearful phenomena of the present day, that we have amongst
us men of high intellect, well-mannered, agreeable, able to inform our minds on matters of high
interest with regard to the visible world and its
forces and arrangements, and yet who make it
their business purposely to infuse doubts about
the Christian faith into the minds of those who
are so unwary as to listen to their fallacies.   These
men have been deceived into thinking that religion
in some way or other interferes with scientific
truth.   Nothing can be more incorrect.   The
province of religion is totally different.   Its sole
object is to induce men to repent of their sins,
and live to the glory of God.   Yet by a strange
hallucination Satan has conjured up an unnatural
aversion amongst men of science, against the pure
and holy law of God and His Son Jesus Christ.
It behoves all serious Christians themselves to
beware, and to warn their brethren against this
    st fearful evil of modern days.

CHAPTER XIV.

PHILOSOPHERS—some philosophers, I should say, have a very odd habit. When they come to anything which they do not know, they fancy that nobody else knows it—and declare it is " unknowable !" So when they have perplexed their brains about some matter, till they are fairly puzzled, they declare the thing is " unthinkable ;" when all the while the matter which perplexes them may be perfectly thinkable, and knowable, and, in fact, very well known to most other persons. The simple reason is that they have put from them the means by which others have acquired their knowledge, and adopted some method of their own. These persons might know as well as other people if they would but use their common understanding, and listen to the instruction of those whom GOD has sent to teach them. " The phenomena of matter and force," says Professor

Tyndall,[1] " lie within our intellectual range, and
as far as they reach we will at all hazards push
our inquiries. But behind, and above, and
around all, the real mystery of the universe lies
unsolved, and so far as we are concerned, is incapable of solution." This may be said in
humility, lamenting the circumscribed limits of
the philosopher's intellectual range, or it may
imply that what is beyond these limits is unknown
and unknowable.

Such philosophers as I have described declare
that they do not know GOD and cannot know
Him. GOD to them is " Unknown and Unknowable." I do not wonder it should be so. I do not
see how it is likely that philosophers—*mere* philosophers who are nothing else, could expect to know
GOD. They have no means of knowing Him, for
they seek Him altogether in a wrong way. " The
world by wisdom knows not GOD." Do they
think that by the help of the telescope they can
discern GOD seated on a throne above the clouds ?
or dwelling amongst the far off stars ? Do they
imagine that the microscope will reveal to them
some subtle all-pervading substance which is
GOD ? Do they suppose that He is some yet un-
discovered element, to be classed with carbon, or
oxygen, or hydrogen, or ozone, or iodine—some
gas, some metal ? For these are the sort of things

[1] Fragments of Science, p. 93.

with which our modern philosophers are conversant—of the spiritual world they know nothing.
" Some have not the knowledge of GOD; I speak
this to your shame." Or do they suppose that
imagination will help them to discover the Great
First Cause and Artificer of the Universe? Nay,
they deny that there is any such being. All that
imagination has yet taught them is, some fate or
settled order of nature, not a being at all, or if he
be so, yet so inert and helpless that it matters not
whether he exist or not.

It is most true that the finite intellect of man
cannot fully comprehend the Infinite GOD. To
use an illustration which, inadequate as it is, may
yet serve to explain the matter, the relation of
GOD to His creatures is something like the relation of a parent to his children ; a child knows
that his parents love him, and take care of him,
and provide for his wants and punish him if he is
naughty, and that in some way he belongs to
them ; but he knows very little, next to nothing
in fact, of what they really are, and what are
their thoughts and occupations in this world.
His father may be a great philosopher, whose
occupation is to investigate the nature of distant
worlds, or the mysteries of animal life. But of
all this the child knows nothing. Or he may be
a bishop, or a general officer, or a member of
Parliament. But the child comprehends nothing

of all these things. Perhaps his father may
be a surgeon, and have to cut off people's
legs and arms, or perhaps he may be a judge and
have to send people to prison, or order them for
execution. All this would seem to the child very
cruel when he is first told of it, simply because he
is entirely ignorant of the real circumstances of
the case. Just as though we know GOD as our
Father and Preserver, we know comparatively
little of His government of the universe, and
some things appear to us inexplicable, perhaps
even unjust.

I have often thought how impossible it is for
us to know what is the real extent of the world
of intellect. For all we know this world may be
but one of millions of worlds, all of which but
this one miserable world may have retained their
allegiance to their great Creator, and have never
fallen from righteousness. The amount of sin and
misery in this earth is enormous in itself, but
comparatively it may be as one of the stars in
heaven compared with the multitude of the
heavenly host. This poor world may be the only
spot in creation where Satan is able to contend
for the mastery over the souls of intelligent beings.
And this is only one of the multitude of moral
and spiritual circumstances relating to GOD's
government, of which we are profoundly ignorant.

While admitting our ignorance of GOD in many
parts of His infinite kingdom, and in respect to
His eternal essence, still, in all that relates to
ourselves, and our own duties and interests, it is
very far from true to say that we know not GOD.
How do we know any one—any one whom we have
not seen face to face? We know him by his works,
his character; we know him by the communica-
tions which we have had with him, and he with
us, or by the report which others have brought of
him.

First, we know GOD by report, or, as we should
say, Revelation. Revelation, says the sceptic,
with a sneer, I would not give much for the information derived from that source. But listen.
Suppose there should be a great debate, as indeed
there has been, whether the distant stars are inhabited worlds like ours or not. A great deal might be
said by way of reasoning on both sides; but it is
evident that no certainty could be obtained. The
subject is not within our cognizance. But suppose a messenger were to come down from one of
the stars and tell us, from his own knowledge,
that it really was inhabited. Then clearly our
only concern would be to make sure that the
messenger had actually come from thence. Having
ascertained that fact, we should receive on his
authority what we could not possibly learn from
any reasoning of our own. This would be faith.

The Christian by Revelation knows GOD to be the Maker of heaven and earth, and all that therein is. He knows that in the beginning GOD created the heaven and earth—that GOD said "Let there be light, and there was light"—that it was GOD Who made the sun to rule the day, and the moon to rule the night. He made the stars also—those wonderful orbs of light, and probably of life, which stud the heavens. He knows Who made them all, and maintains them in their course. He knows GOD as the Creator of all things living, Who breathed into man a living soul, and created him in His own image, and spake to him, and bade him be lord over the rest of creation. He knows him, also, as revealed in the New Covenant—the SAVIOUR and Redeemer of mankind. He knows Him as his Sanctifier and Comforter—the power by Whom alone he can live a life of righteousness and happiness. He knows, moreover, that He will come at the last day to be his Judge—that He has prepared a place for those who love and serve Him; and, alas! a place also for those who know Him not. What can we desire to know more of GOD; what could we expect to know that GOD has not revealed to us? What, with our present faculties, are we capable of knowing which GOD has not declared? The time, indeed, will come when those who have believed what GOD has revealed

to them now, will see GOD as He is, and know
Him even as they are known. It is a great and
glorious thought to believe that when this poor
life is over we shall be admitted into the glorious
presence of the Almighty, and behold all the
wonders of His creation and government; see, as
He sees, the wonderful mechanism of the heavens,
know what is the nature of the far-off stars, and
the planets which form our system, whether they
are habitable or no, what kind of beings dwell
there: how it is that the sun pours forth its in-
terminable stream of light and heat, and yet is
not consumed, and what is scarcely less wonderful, discern the less than microscopic creatures
which people this earth which we inhabit, and all
the chemical agencies and forces which surround
the elements of matter—and still more, the moral
government of the great Ruler, how He controls
the spiritual agency, whether of men and angels,
and wields by His sole will the thoughts and
actions of the beings whom He has made. All
this insight into nature's greatest mysteries will
be part of the reward of those who love GOD.

It has sometimes occurred to me what must be the
blank disappointment of the sceptical philosopher
who has forfeited his place in heaven, when he
arrives at another world. He has been one who
in this world has set his whole mind on scientific
discoveries, enlarged, it may be, the knowledge of

his age—one who is admired and looked up to as
foremost in his department. Up to the very last
he has been engaged heart and soul in his favourite pursuit, but with little thought of his spiritual
life, and prejudiced against the truth as it is in
CHRIST. Some fatal accident, or a few days'
illness, have cut short his career—his body is laid
in the grave, his portrait, it may be, is given to
the world—his biography written by some admiring disciple—and his spirit is departed—whither?
I remember a short time ago it was recorded in
the biography of some man of science—I am far
from saying that his was the case which I have
supposed—but one saying was recorded of him,
that in the midst of health and life he had declared that he would willingly die that moment
if he might be allowed to return to life some 500
years hence, and some one might be appointed to
explain to him all the scientific discoveries which
had been made in the meantime. One can well
imagine that, perhaps, the greatest reward of the
Christian philosopher, who in the eager pursuit
of science, has not lost sight of his hope in
CHRIST, one of the greatest rewards imaginable
in another world would be to be made acquainted
with the wonders of creation—to have many
things made clear to him, which in this world he
had vainly endeavoured to discover, and, above
all, to know GOD as He is. And if one can well

imagine the joy and gratitude which the discovery
of nature's great secrets would be to the philosopher who believed in CHRIST, what must be the
abject despair of the sceptic or unbeliever, who
with the same high philosophical aspirations,
found, when he awoke from the grave, that, for
his sin and unbelief, he had forfeited all hope of
increasing his knowledge, and was condemned to
remain in doubt and darkness for ever.

I can imagine a case, which in some slight
degree might illustrate the misery of such an one.
Suppose that two hundred years ago there lived
in France a statesman high in position, whose
whole heart and soul were occupied in State in-
trigues and policy—one able to guide the helm of
the State, and influence the affairs of nations. In
an evil hour this man has committed himself, we
will say, to some treasonable affair, has been discovered, arrested, and thrown into the Bastile for
life. Perhaps "the man with the iron mask" may
have been such an one. He is shut up within
the narrow walls of a dungeon, where scarce a ray
of light finds entrance. Perhaps a single gleam
slowly traverses the wall of his prison each day,
making the darkness only more visible. For
weary days and nights he wears out his monoto-
nous existence. His keeper brings him his daily
food, but speaks no word in answer to his eager
inquiries—he can obtain no information respect-

M

ing the outer world. All the schemes in which
his mind was formerly so deeply interested have
passed as a shadow—to him they are as though
they never had been. He hears the crowd passing
by his prison walls, sometimes he notes the march
of armed men—sometimes the shout of the multitude which once greeted him as he passed—his
restless mind perplexes itself to discover the
meaning of the sounds he hears—but to no avail.
Days, months, and years pass on. At last the
interests of the world gradually die away—he
comes to acknowledge that to him they are as
nothing—the pageantry of the world has passed
away.

Something like this we may conceive to be the
case of the scientific infidel, cast into outer darkness, debarred for his sin from taking further interest in the pursuits in which his soul delighted.
Only in one point the parallel holds not. The
politician doomed to pass his life in a dungeon,
excluded from the interests of the world, may set
his mind on higher things, and for CHRIST's sake
obtain pardon in heaven. The sceptic who has
died in his unbelief is doomed for ever to a fate
of everlasting ignorance. GOD was unknown to
him in this life, and will remain unknowable for
ever.

It is a strange notion to exhort philosophers to
believe in GOD, and serve Him, in order that after

this life they may be admitted to a knowledge of
all the deep mysteries of nature which now per-
plex them ; yet I know not that any motive is to
be rejected which might draw men to GOD.
Certàinly the fear of being shut out for ever from
all hope in advancing in the path of science, may
well be classed among the terrors of the LORD,
and the certainty of such a result of a course of
sin and unbelief seems undeniable.

I will end my chapter with one of Chalmers'
splendid passages.   "Oh, it is a deeply interesting spectacle to behold a man, who can take a
masterly and commanding survey over the field
of some human speculation ; who can clear his
discriminated way through all the turns and in-
genuities of human argument ; who by the march
of mighty and restless demonstrations, can scale
with assured footsteps the sublimities of science,
and from the firm stand on the eminence he has
won, can descry some wondrous range of natural
or intellectual truth spread out in subordination
before him.   And yet this very man may, in
reference to the moral and authoritative claims of
the Godhead, be in a state of utter apathy and
blindness ! All his attempts, either at the spiritual
discernment, or the practical impression of this
doctrine, may be arrested and baffled by the
weight of some inexplicable impotency.   A man
of homely talents, and still homelier education,

may see what *he* cannot see, and feel what *he* cannot feel; and wise and prudent as he is, there may lie the barrier of an obstinate and impenetrable concealment, between his accomplished mind, and those things which are revealed unto babes." [1]

[1] See " Discourses on Christian Revelation viewed in connection with Modern Astronomy," p. 247.

CHAPTER XV.

THE astronomers of ancient days, although they had not invented telescopes, yet made no inconsiderable advance in science—albeit entirely on a wrong principle. The system of astronomy most in vogue was the Ptolemaic system. The astronomers of those times did not know that the sun was the centre of the planetary system; at least, they did not believe it, though Pythagoras had taught it long before. The earth was in their view the chief object in creation. They fancied that it was a vast immoveable horizontal plain, and that the sun moved upwards in the heavens, as it seems to move each morning, and went down at evening below the western horizon; and the moon and the planets (for they were very accurate observers) appeared to them to perform certain cycles and epicycles in the heavens, which they noted down with the greatest precision. More-

over, they invented the signs of the zodiac, and
mapped out the heavens in a number of constel-
lations, to which they gave fantastic names, the
Great Bear, the Little Bear, Orion, Capricorn—
most of which for convenience' sake have been
retained in the present day.   They were even
able to calculate eclipses, and, in fact, made as-
tonishingly clever attempts at explaining the re-
volutions of the heavenly bodies.   But they were
all wrong; and that, simply because they did not
know that the sun was the true centre of the
system.   At last Copernicus taught them the
solution.   Thenceforth with the sun for their
centre, all the various motions of the earth, the
moon and planets, were developed in due order,
and are seen to constitute one vast majestic whole.

And it is remarkable that the very discovery of
the grandeur of the heavenly system, has but served
to show us our own littleness.   Instead of the
earth being, as was before supposed, the greatest
object of creation, and all the heavenly host created
to be subservient to us, we find that we are but
a speck, as it were, in the ocean of infinity.

Thus the sun is the greatest material power in
our planetary system.   And so in the moral universe, GOD is the sun of our system from which
all spiritual light is evolved, and not light only,
but all spiritual force, and power, and motion.
GOD is the centre of the great moral and intel-

lectual universe—moving, directing, enlightening
all things. To construct a theory of human affairs, a system of ethics or philosophy, and to
ignore the moving and enlightening powers of
God, is like going back to the Ptolemaic system
of astronomy, and supposing the earth to be the
centre of the universe. No doubt many clever
guesses might be made by persons holding such
a theory—just as the ancient astronomers, considering their ignorance of the moving principle,
made many ingenious calculations. But such
notions would be vague and erratic; such a system barren and imperfect. The moral world
would be to these modern atheists one great flat.
Philosophers who held this notion might, no doubt,
calculate and trace a good many of the common
operations of the human mind, and the course of
human events, as the old astronomers traced the
course of the planets on their imperfect hypothesis: they might trace the progress of civilization, or imagine they had traced it—how science
grew up, and art, and culture. Ignorant of the
existence of a great and beneficent Creator, they
might imagine the state of the world when men
were developed out of monkeys, and began to
make flint-heads to arrows, and lived in mud
cabins, and how they advanced from the mud
cabin to the castle and the palace, from skins of
beasts for their clothing to silks and cottons

They might form their speculations, and suppose
some law of nature by which these things pro-
gressed.   Shrewd guesses, too, they might make
as to the probable course of human events—just
as the old astronomers made their cycles and
epicycles.   But without the light of GOD's Providence all would be vague, doubtful, and misty.
The origin, the true position, and final destiny of
man would be an enigma to them without GOD—
mere random guess-work or laborious drivelling.
GOD is the true central power of human affairs,
the light of the moral, as the sun is of the material
world.   What a tangled and perplexing scene is
this world, what cycles and endless epicycles are
there if we eliminate from it the central moving
power of GOD's Providence, ruling and directing
all things.

Thus, as the sun is the centre of light and heat
to the visible world—so to the moral world, to the
nations and families of the world "GOD is light."
"GOD is love."   It is a bold thing for us to speak
of the nature and essence of the great Eternal
Spirit, the Ruler of heaven and earth, but under
the guidance of the Inspired Word we may at
least gather some portion of this mysterious truth.
What then is the nature of GOD?   "GOD is a
Spirit, and they that worship Him must worship
Him in spirit and in truth."   "In Him we live,
and move, and have our being."   Again, "GOD

is love," and yet again, " Our GOD is a consuming
fire." How is this ? How can He Whose essence
is love be also a consuming fire ? Even as the
sun which is the fountain of genial warmth—can
scorch, and burn up, and destroy. GOD is indeed a GOD of love to those who love and obey
Him. His love is infinite. " In this was manifested the love of GOD towards us, in that He
sent His Only-Begotten SON into the world, that
we might live by Him." " Herein is love, not
that we loved GOD, but that He loved us, and
sent His SON to be the propitiation for our sins."
Is it possible to conceive greater love than this ?
GOD loves us all, He desires to raise each one of
us to be with Him for ever in glory. He has
done everything that could be done, even in the
sacrifice of His dear SON. But if we reject His
love—if we continue in sin and hard-hearted unbelief, and refuse to listen to His voice of kindness—then " our GOD is a consuming fire."

Again, GOD is light. This attribute of GOD, if
it be an attribute, and not, as love, the essence of
His nature, appears to include not only infinite
power, wisdom, and goodness, but the idea also of
clearness, beauty, glory, intelligence, all the highest graces of the intellect. GOD is light, and in
Him is no darkness at all. What the light of
the sun is to the visible world, that is GOD to the
spiritual. Imagine the world without light,

wrapped in a mantle of gloom and darkness, as it
was in times of old before the habitation of man
was prepared, when the earth was without form,
and void, and darkness was upon the face of the
deep. Then, we read, "the Spirit of GOD moved
upon the face of the waters, and GOD said, 'Let
there be light:' and there was light." Picture to
yourselves the change which at that word took
place. Earth, and sky, and sea lit up with the
new creation. What just before was dull, and
dead, and lifeless, is now clothed in varied colours
reflected from sea, and cloud, and azure sky. And
such as light is to the material world, such is GOD
to the world of spirits. Without Him, without
the grace of His Spirit, all is gloomy, and deso-
late, and dark. But when the Spirit of GOD has
breathed upon man's moral nature, then spring
up all the graces of the Spirit—love, joy, peace,
gentleness, meekness, charity, all the noble virtues which adorn the spirit of man; all the
amiable and gentle qualities which warm the
heart—faith, hope, charity; all these spring from
the presence of GOD, Who is the light of the soul
—the centre and origin of all that is good and
lovely.

And GOD is light in that He is the source and
centre of all intelligence—all the multiplied attainments of the human intellect derive their
power from Him, and are exercised on the objects

which He has created. And yet there are those who imagine that this world could go on without the intervention of a personal GOD, and would eliminate GOD from His own creation! You might as well take away the sun from the centre of the planetary system. Not more vague and irregular would be the system in which we live, robbed of its central sun, than would be the course of the moral world without GOD as its Prime Mover and Controller.

GOD is light, the Light of the world, in that His revealed Truth is the grand source of all our knowledge of spiritual things. Through many ages of spiritual darkness in which the nations of the earth were immersed, yea even civilized and philosophical nations, not only was the true GOD unknown, but men were given over to horrible crimes and vile affections,—in all this time there was one people, the chosen people of GOD, amongst whom the true GOD was known, and many holy men lived and died whose inspired writings even now shed light and life amongst us. The Psalms of David, the Proverbs of Solomon, the sublime effusions of the old Prophets far surpass the moral and spiritual effusions of the rest of the ancient world. It is a strange thing that out of the ignorance of those early days, a nation should spring up like that of Israel, which should in many things be acknowledged as the instructor and schoolmaster of the civilized nations of modern Europe. Yet so it was.

Then in the fulness of the time came CHRIST into the world, "the true Light, which lighteth every man that cometh into the world."

We cannot tell why it was that GOD so long delayed the coming of His SON—unless it was to prove how incapable was man, even when advanced in intellectual cultivation, to attain to moral excellence without direct communication from the source of light. " As many as received Him, to them gave He power to become the sons of GOD, even to them that believe in His name."

The Gospel of CHRIST specially reveals to us GOD as a GOD of love—not only of purity and holiness, but of mercy and loving-kindness. When we read of the state of society amongst the most civilized nations of antiquity, when we think of the ancient Romans with all their grandeur gloating over the cruel sports of the amphitheatre, watching the life-blood flowing from the breast of the dying gladiator, when we think of the grossness of their lives, cruelty, and impurity, not less shocking than that which called down fire from heaven on the cities of the plain, we can discern that mere intellectual culture alone had no efficacy to soften the heart, or promote purity and holiness. The doctrine of CHRIST, and the kindly, gentle influence which He diffused among the nations might indeed be called light springing up in darkness.

There are those who attribute the greater refinement of men's manners in the present day to civilization. Yes, but they forget that modern civilization is in truth the offspring of Christianity. But for Christianity we should be no better than the old Romans, proud, cruel, inexorable, savage in heart, however refined and noble in manner. It is Christianity which has introduced those gentle, heavenly graces which, in those who truly receive them, are able to subdue the gross and violent passions of the human heart, and render them gentle and holy.

Never was there a greater mistake than to suppose that any real contrast exists between the pure Christian faith, and the attainments of modern civilization and science. Why should not the man of science be a Christian? Why should not the Christian be a man of science? Oh, let us not imagine that there is any antagonism between the GOD of nature, and the GOD of Revelation. Let us believe that GOD is light and love in the natural as in the spiritual world, and only strive with each other which shall render Him the worthiest homage. It is sin and unbelief that separate us from the GOD of light and love— irreligion, impurity, unbelief, worldliness. These are truly works of darkness—they wrap the soul in gloom, shut out the brightness of GOD's presence, intercept the rays of divine love, make men hard, and cruel, and selfish. Let us put from us these works of darkness and walk as children of light. Then shall we learn to see Him as He is, and discern the beauty of His holiness, and appreciate the infinity of His love. Then will all His ways appear to us holy, just, and good,—doubts and difficulties will disappear from our vision, and we shall know Him as a GOD of light and love. Some there are who positively hate the Gospel of CHRIST,—the proud, the self-willed, who cannot bear to be controlled and thwarted,—those who are living in known sin which the Gospel tells them that they must give up, but they will not; those who see with envy its influences; those who feel that they have wilfully excluded themselves from the pale of its blessings. Alas! to them the Gospel is no blessing. The light is shining around them, but they choose darkness rather than light; the bright fountain of living water flows freely, but they will not drink of it; the Bread of Life is prepared for them, but they will not eat of it. They are starving in the midst of plenty, grovelling in darkness while light is shining around.

Others there are to whom the blessed Gospel is an atmosphere of light shining round about them, in the midst of a dark and dreary world.

Is it not a glorious privilege to live in the sunshine of GOD's light and love,—to know GOD as our FATHER, JESUS CHRIST as our Redeemer, the HOLY GHOST as our Sanctifier? Is it not a blessed privilege to enter GOD's House, to know that He is there to hear us, to have no doubt that He is listening to us, as we pour forth our praises and supplications? All these things the faithful see, and hear, and are sure of. The eye of faith discerns things spiritual, as the natural eye discerns material things, and has no doubt about them, any more than when we see the sun shining in his splendour. As in ancient days the Egyptians were plagued with a darkness which might be felt, while the children of Israel had light in their dwellings, so it is now; the worldly and the wicked see nothing of the glory of spiritual things, they grope about in darkness— a gross oppressive darkness which entangles them in its folds, and limits their sight to the world's narrow horizon, beyond which all is gloomy and undefined. GOD, and the things of GOD, are to them "unknown and unknowable," while the children of light, walking in the sunshine of the Gospel of light and love, enjoy the continual light of GOD's countenance,—know that He is looking down upon them, and loveth them as a father loveth his children.

CHAPTER XVI.

THERE are many semi-religious, semi-philosophi-
cal questions which arise in the minds of those
who think on the state of the world. Some are
beyond our present understanding, and must
remain undecided till we enter upon another state
of existence. Some are not so difficult. It perplexes many persons to see so much evil, and
unhappiness, and injustice as exists all around us
in the world. They are at a loss to know why all
this should be suffered. To mere philosophers it
is natural enough that such difficulties should
arise. They have not any principle to account
for what they see. But the Christian has no
misgivings about it. The Christian believes in
the absolute power of the Almighty as Ruler of
the universe. He believes that everything is
ordered by GOD's absolute Will, and yet that
GOD *can* do nothing unjust. How is this? It

is impossible that He should oppress or deal un-
kindly with His people, because not only is His
power absolute, but also His goodness and His
wisdom are infinite. His absolute goodness prevents Him from doing wrong or injustice in His
government of His people, and His absolute
Wisdom insures His doing what is right. Hence
the Christian has no doubts or misgivings in
regard to the government of the affairs of the
world ; he feels sure that all is in the hands of an
Almighty, all-wise, and all-merciful GOD and
FATHER, who will distribute justice throughout
His dominion. There may be many things in
the affairs of the world which the Christian cannot account for—many things in the Bible which
appear difficult to comprehend—many things in
history which are beyond his understanding—
nay, many things actually existing which are full
of perplexity. But believing, or rather knowing,
that there is a divine and holy Providence ruling
over all, he is not disturbed or doubtful. He is
fully persuaded that all things work together for
eventual good.

The objector will say, If GOD has absolute
power over all things in the world, why does He
not annihilate and stamp out the evil which
exists ? The answer is, that this evil arises from
man's liberty of action. It is impossible to
stamp out the evil without destroying the free

N

will of man, or man himself. God did once stamp
out the evil when He destroyed one whole generation by the waters of the flood. Would we
desire that He should continually from time to
time destroy the world in like manner ? It matters not whether we think it would be best or
not. He has declared that He will not again
destroy the world until the last great day. And
meanwhile by the most wondrous exhibition of
mingled power and goodness He seeks to bring
back His erring sons to their allegiance.

But there are some passages of Holy Scripture
in which God seems to have permitted or even
encouraged wrong doing. The answer to this difficulty is not far to seek. God never causes sinfulness in man; He allows the use of free will to
all, and He uses the sinfulness and evil passion
of wicked men for His good purposes. And
these are chiefly two: first, to punish other evil
doers ; secondly, to try the spirit of His saints
and bring them to greater excellence. How many
instances might be quoted in which the sinfulness
and evil passions of wicked men have been employed for the punishment of other wicked men.
God did not make Nebuchadnezzar a tyrant and
an oppressor, but He made use of his tyranny to
punish His people who had rebelled against Him.
God did not make Judas treacherous and covetous, nor Pontius Pilate unjust and timeserving ;

but He availed Himself of the evil qualities of
these men to accomplish His great design for the
salvation of mankind. There are a thousand
instances in the Bible in which the Almighty
Ruler thus makes use of the sinfulness of man,
whether to accomplish His judgments on the
wicked, or to try the constancy of His saints, or
otherwise work out the designs of His good
Providence; just as he might employ a lion, or a
whirlwind, or drought, or pestilence. And surely
we can see the same Providence still working in
these our days. God did not cause the political
jealousies between the Northern and Southern
states of America, but He employed their evil passions to work out the emancipation of three or
four millions of slaves. He did not put into the
hearts of the Communists of Paris the furious and
evil passions by which they were actuated; but
employed their violence to chastise a luxurious
and immoral people, and to afford warning to
other nations, if they will but heed it. So, now
it is not God who has caused the covetousness
and self-will which prevails amongst us in England, nor the infidelity and atheism with which
our unhappy land is infested; yet it is well if
He do not make these evil qualities the instruments of His Providence to punish and chastise us.

Some persons are disturbed by the fulfilment

of prophecy. They imagine that if GOD brings to pass the prophecies which He has caused His servants to deliver, He must needs be the author of the crimes and violence by which in many cases the prophecies were fulfilled. But this is to take a wrong view of the matter. GOD may foresee what will happen, and yet not be the cause of it. Even we ourselves may often foresee the course which events will take—or the mode in which men will act. If we know the character of a man, we may be able to predict with tolerable accuracy how he will act under given circum-stances. We can tell how he will vote. We can predict whether he will act nobly or meanly, honestly or dishonestly. But seeing that GOD has a perfect knowledge of what is in man, and of all the circumstances in which he will be placed, He is able to foresee with certainty what will be the course of events, and that without interfering with them, but simply suffering the will of man to have its way. At the same time, as we have already seen, it is perfectly compatible with the justice and goodness of GOD to avail Himself of the will and actions of men to bring to pass the events of His good providence.

And amongst all the troubles and evils of the present world there is one certain fact on which the Christian takes his stand, and from which he rives a settled confidence. Not only has he a

perfect faith in the goodness and wisdom of God
—but he believes and knows with a knowledge
as certain as anything can be known that this
life and all that we see around us in this present
world is a part only, and a comparatively small
part of the dispensation of God's Providence.
There is a world to come in which the inequali-
ties and injustice, and evil which exist here will
all be remedied and set right. He has not the
slightest doubt that they who fear the Lord will
have a happy portion hereafter; joy in heaven
which will abundantly compensate for all the
trials of this life. In this respect the Christian
has an immense advantage over the unbeliever.
The vision of the unbeliever is limited to the
narrow horizon of the present world. His philosophy is circumscribed within the straitest bounds.
He lacks the clue to all that is noblest and most
intellectual. The mere philosopher is conversant
with nothing nobler or more important than the
material universe with its component parts. He
is altogether ignorant of the world of spirits—of
the spiritual state of man, his capacities and
powers. Think only of the astonishing truths
with which the Christian is conversant, from the
revelation of Scripture and from the writings of
the ablest men of the last eighteen hundred years,
who have devoted the whole faculties of their
souls to the elucidation of the ways of God to

man. Why, the very poorest man who has been
educated at a village school, and has attended his
church regularly, really knows more of the highest
truths of intellectual and spiritual life than the
greatest philosopher whose days have been spent
amidst the wonders of natural science, but who is
ignorant of Spiritual Truth. It is admitted on
all hands that in the present age science has
reached a point of development far higher than
any which the world had before arrived at. It
must necessarily be so: because the discoveries
of one age serve as the foundation on which to
build an ever-increasing fabric. Sometimes indeed
a theory, which has been confidently asserted, is
found to be without foundation. Perhaps some
which at present occupy the minds of philosophers
may be found to be of this character. Such
theories of course are set aside by increased knowledge. But speaking generally the present generation stands on a lofty eminence of scientific
knowledge. But after all what is the value of
this knowledge, if they who have acquired it do at
the same time let slip the knowledge of GOD—of
Spiritual Truth ? It is well to know the revolution of the planets and the mechanism of distant
worlds, but what is that in comparison with the
knowledge of the great Architect of the universe ?
It is well to know the forces of nature, and the
structure of the animal frame, and all the vast

variety of organic matter; but what is this when
compared with the world of spirits, the method
of GOD's dealing with the souls of men, the way
in which we may render an acceptable service to
our Maker, our Redeemer, our Sanctifier ? What
wonderful depths and heights of knowledge are
comprised in the Revelation which GOD has
given us of His Will, His Nature, His Attributes
—the combination of justice and mercy with
which He deals with the souls of men. Surely
all this is infinitely beyond any possible discovery
in the realm of mere material science ! We may
surely say with Venerable Bede—

> " Qui Christum noscit sat scit si cætera nescit :
> Qui Christum nescit nil scit si cætera noscit."[1]

But after all why not know both ? There is no
real antagonism between the knowledge of GOD
and of His works: nay, rather the Christian philosopher who knows GOD and His works is the
only true philosopher.

[1] Quoted from the *Guardian*, May 29th, 1873.

CHAPTER XVII.

IT is difficult to understand how clever men, or even men of common sense can imagine that it is according to reason to deny the existence of the supernatural in the face of the testimony by which the occurrence of supernatural events has been substantiated. The only argument is, that they themselves have never witnessed any supernatural occurrence. It reminds one of the man who was accused of some misdemeanour and informed that several witnesses had seen him do what he was accused of. "For every witness," said he, "that says he saw me do it, I can bring forward a dozen that did not see me." Surely philosophers must know that it is impossible to prove a negative in the face of many positive witnesses of a fact. If twelve men declare that they saw with their own eyes the supernatural works of our LORD, it matters not how many did not see Him, or do not think them probable. You may have a strong opinion that a thing is not likely : but if the fact is proved, your *a priori* opinion goes for nothing.

A distinction should be drawn, though it is not easy always to maintain it—between the supernatural and the preternatural. The supernatural is something above the actually constituted order of nature—the preternatural is something beyond or contrary to it. The supernatural is the authority which GOD exercises over nature whether to establish or control it—the preternatural is something different from GOD's supernatural government—the miraculous in fact.

Now it is self-evident that there have been many very great deviations from the original state of things. No one supposes that the world has been going on just as it is from eternity. There must have been a beginning, and if so, there must have been some power which first set in motion what we now see around us, and the act of doing so must have been supernatural, that is, something above the state of things which then existed. Once there was a time when all the things which we see did not exist. So far all agree. As S. Paul says: "By faith we understand that the worlds were framed by the Word of GOD, so that those things which are seen, were not made of things which do appear." But the creation of the rude materials of this visible world was of

less marvellous character than the creation of the
various accessories which we see about it—light,
heat, electricity, gravitation, chemical affinity—
all the apparatus for causing rain, and wholesome atmosphere, and the growth of vegetation,
and the variety of circumstances which are necessary for the sustentation of life. And then came
the still greater work of peopling the earth with
living inhabitants, when the sea, the air, the
earth, were all made to teem with animal life,
which did not before exist. And lastly, God
created man in His own image, endowed with
moral sense, reason, and immortality. The very
bringing into existence of what we consider now
to be perfectly natural, yet must have been at first
a supernatural act. Even the creation of a monad
would be a supernatural act, and involve the po-
tentiality of any number of future supernatural
acts. It is obvious that the Power which could
first make a monad from which creation was to be
evolved, might have made all the same creatures
at several times, and not only an original monad.
In fact, it seems a great deal more difficult to
conceive the creation of this wonderful monad,
than to believe in the creation of separate creatures. To many minds the monad would be
simply " unthinkable."

If there be one fact more clearly established
than another by the discoveries of modern science

it is that the earth existed for a vast period
of time before man lived upon it. In truth, it
was for many ages in such a state of rudeness
and confusion that man could not have lived if
he had been placed in it. The discoveries of
science agree remarkably with the description of
the earth when it was without form and void, and
darkness was upon the face of the waters. How
could man live without light? GOD first made
the materials of the world, then prepared it for
man to live upon it, then created him to be its
lord and master. And whenever He created him,
and however, if, as some philosophers say, He
made him out of a gorilla, it must have been by
a supernatural act. This one fact, the creation
of man with his wonderful and fearful structure,
not of body only but of mind, his power of reasoning, his capacity for goodness; this one fact,
if there were not a thousand others, proves to us
beyond a question, that there is a great and
mighty and intelligent Spirit Who controls the
universe, and governs it according to His good
will; and though it may be true as a general rule
that things go on in a regular settled order—an
order settled and appointed by Him—yet that He
has the power, as He has shown also that He has
the will, to deviate from the settled order of
things, and do what is supernatural, even to
the extent of creating the visible universe, and

so wonderful a creature as man, appears self-evident.

It would seem then that the creation of man was the great object and design of GOD's previous arrangement—that the world was originally created, and afterwards prepared for man's use, and that, so far at least as the system of this one planet is concerned, everything was designed and constituted in order that it should be the habitation and trial place of man.

It is evident also that He Who created could also destroy. Man even can destroy what he has made. He who builds a house can pull it down; he who plants a tree can root it up. It is unquestionable therefore that GOD can change or re-arrange or modify as He chooses what He has created. The records which we have of GOD's miraculous dispensations have no improbability whatever on the score of lack of power on GOD's part to do what He will with what He has created. And as man was the great object of creation, so far as we are cognisant of it, so man is the great object of the different dispensations by which GOD has wrought changes in His work. If GOD did, as we are assured, place man in Paradise in order that he might enjoy happiness so long as he was obedient to His law, we can easily understand and appreciate GOD's motive for interference when, on man's disobedience He

drove him from his blest abode, and placed him
in scenes where he could eat bread in the sweat
of his face. We can understand why, when
many generations of men had arisen, and GOD
saw that the wickedness of man was great upon
the earth, and every imagination of his heart was
only evil continually, He should resolve to destroy
that evil generation by the waters of a Deluge.
I see not that there is the least improbability in
the account which we have of this great event.
The improbability would be if the Mighty Power
which first made the universe and man did *not*
interfere in its concerns. The creation of the
world, the placing of such a being as man upon
it, proves the existence of an Almighty and
All-wise Creator, with power and intelligence
to accomplish whatsoever He wills. When therefore the creatures of His hand to whom He has
given such high endowments, dared to rebel
against Him, what is there strange or incredible
in the course of His proceedings which is recorded?

If it be asked *how* it is that GOD causes supernatural results? the answer is simple. He is
Himself altogether and essentially supernatural,
He is bound by no laws of nature. He may do
what He will by the mere word of His mouth
which is mighty in operation, or He may use the
services of innumerable angels which surround

His throne. We know not *how* it is, but this we
know from our common understanding, that He
Who first created the universe, and established the
laws by which it is governed, must needs, by the
exercise of the same power, be able to change or
to destroy it.

The mere existence of such a being as man
necessarily involves the existence of a Creator
and Preserver. When we consider his high intellectual endowments and capabilities, it is incredible that he should have grown up out of
inert or unintelligent matter without the intervention of a superior intelligence, first to conceive,
then to create him. And when we see his lamentable moral weakness, it seems equally improbable
that there should be no one, so to speak, to look
after him, to help and to guide him, in one word,
a Providence. It seems to me a puerile idea
either that the great world and all that is in it
came into existence without the intervention of
a great and beneficent Creator, or that having
made the world, its Creator should neglect to
govern it with His wisdom. All real philosophy
is based on the great truth that GOD is everywhere present guiding and controlling the work
which He has made. "The eyes of the LORD
are in every place beholding the evil and the
good." "The very hairs of our head are all
numbered, and without Him not a sparrow fall-

eth to the ground." "Can any one hide himself in secret places that I shall not see him? Do I not fill heaven and earth?"

God's Omnipresence is perhaps the grandest idea not only of religion but of philosophy. His all-seeing eye is over us watching us with anxious care, about our path by day, and about our bed by night, to guard, protect and bless us. He watches with benevolent interest to see how we employ the existence which He has given us, how we cultivate our reason, and control our high powers and affections and faculties which He has bestowed. He is grieved if He sees the creatures of His hand abusing His excellent gifts, just as a good father grieves for the misconduct of a beloved son. And when He sees that we desire to please Him, imperfect though our attempts may be, He views them with kind indulgence, and helps our infirmities, and sustains our faltering steps. This may be anthropomorphism, but it is all the same a blessed and a holy truth.

But still deeper and holier is the feeling if we go on to consider the peculiar doctrines of the Christian faith. CHRIST dwelling by His Spirit in the hearts of His children. Our hearts the very temples of the HOLY GHOST. Yes, He is very near to those who are His. His Spirit mingles with theirs. We are one with Him, and He with us.

But I will not here enter into the deep mysteries of CHRIST. This is not the time and place. I have only now alluded to them that any one who reads may judge which is noblest, holiest, truest, the Church's doctrine of the supernatural Omnipresence of GOD, and the indwelling of His Spirit, and union of the SAVIOUR; or the notion that man grew up out of a monad without a Creator, and lives and dies without a SAVIOUR.

P.S.—I must protest against the classing such so-called supernatural events as the vision of Marie Marguerite Alacoque at Paray le Monial with the miracles of the New Testament. The latter are attested by many witnesses who laid down their lives in testimony of their sincerity, the other rests only on the unsupported testimony of an apparently hysterical woman. To attempt to class one with the other is on the face of it an entirely unfair and illogical proceeding.

CHAPTER XVIII.

PERSONALITY OF THE EVIL ONE.—PHILOSOPHERS UNABLE
TO EXPLAIN THE MATTER.—THE BIBLE DECLARES IT.

ONE of the subjects on which philosophers differ in
opinion from divines is the existence of a personal
Evil Spirit—the devil, or Satan. It is unfortunate that even good persons, who believe the Bible,
sometimes allow themselves to speak in a banter-
ing tone on the subject, and regard the devil as
an object of ridicule, rather than of dread and
aversion. Certainly if his power and malice be
such as the Bible teaches us, he is no object of
contempt. Let us treat the subject with gravity.

First, divines and philosophers must all admit
with grief that there is an immense mass of sin,
and evil, and mischief of all sorts in the world.
There can be no question about it: so far we are
all agreed.

Well, then, how came the evil to exist? Will
philosophers be so good as to explain to us?
They are unable to do so. Can divines explain
it ? Yes, so far, at least, as the existence of evil

o

in this earth ; the Revelation which God has given
for our instruction explains it fully.   It tells us
first that our first parents were created in the
image of God, that is, as Christians believe, holy,
intellectual, free.   The philosopher, perhaps, will
demur to this statement, and either discard it
altogether, or admit it only as a. myth or allegory.
However, it is impossible to deny that the first
rational and responsible beings must some time or
other have come into existence.   How came these
beings to fall into sin, and to give birth to a race
of beings like themselves ?   The philosopher has
no explanation to give; the divine simply tells
the sad tale which the Bible unfolds.   Let us see
whether it is a probable account.   We accept it,
indeed, as true on the authority of God's Word,
and that is enough for us.   Still, it is well to endeavour to remove any difficulties which may present themselves to the mind of the philosopher.

Let us consider what is the precise point in
question.   It is the existence of a personal being,
called the Devil or Satan.   The question is not
now as to his taking the form of a serpent.   Some
may accept the fact literally ; some may regard it
as an allegory.   It is not logical to say, I do not
believe in the transformation of Satan into a serpent, and, therefore, I do not believe that the
first created responsible beings were tempted by
a personal fiend.   We have to consider whether

the fact of the devil tempting our first parents to
sin is in accordance with our general experience.

To me it appears that nothing is more probable. It seems irrational to suppose that man
would of himself have rebelled against his Maker,
Who had been so kind and bountiful to him, and
given him the enjoyment of so many blessings.
We are led to conclude that he must have acted
by the instigation of some malevolent being, not
himself. It is a shocking characteristic of evil
beings—the desire to lead others into sin. Drunkards are always trying to entice others to join
with them in their revels. Impure persons try
to turn others to the same sin. Unbelievers and
sceptics seem to take a malicious pleasure, or perhaps have a sort of curse laid on them, to be always endeavouring to bring others into the same
unhappy state, and often exercise a cunning and
audacity which prove too successful. So it was
with Satan. The account of his proceeding is
strictly according to our every-day experience.
No sooner did he see our first parents dwelling in
happiness amidst the bowers of Paradise, than he
resolved to compass their ruin. By his wily
speech he persuaded Eve that she might eat of
the forbidden fruit, and yet not surely die—yea,
rather that her intellectual vision would be enlarged, and she would become as GOD, knowing
good and evil. So he deceived her and she fell.

Even if we believe these things to be wrapped in allegory, still they are so wonderfully true to nature, so exactly in accordance with what we see around us every day of the proceedings of the agents of evil, that we feel sure that they must be records of something real.

There is a remarkable passage in the first chapter of the Book of Job in which the transactions of the court of heaven are in a manner unfolded to our view. No one who looks deeply into the present system of the world can fail to discern that in the midst of this wonderful scene, whether we regard the natural or moral aspect of the world, while there is abundant evidence of the power and goodness of the great Ruler of heaven and earth, there are at the same time manifest indications of an Evil Spirit going up and down in the earth, marring God's work, spoiling man's happiness, and inflicting on him miseries innumerable. "There was a day," we read, "when the sons of God came to present themselves to the Lord, and Satan came also among them. And the Lord said unto Satan, 'Whence comest thou?' And Satan answered the Lord, 'From going to and fro in the earth, and from walking up and down in it.' And the Lord said unto Satan, 'Hast thou considered My servant Job, that there is none like him in the earth, a perfect and an upright man, one who feareth God and escheweth

evil ?' And Satan answered the LORD, 'Doth
Job serve GOD for nought ?' " This is a wonderful
passage. Be it an allegory or not, it conveys to
us a clear and forcible representation of the superintending Providence of GOD, of the vigilance
with which He takes cognizance of the different
works assigned to His holy angels, the control
which He exercises over the Power of darkness,
and the limits which He assigns to his evil doings. In short, we see a noble picture of the
LORD Omnipotent sitting on the Throne of His
government, and summoning before Him in Person the powers of heaven and hell to give account
of all that they have done.

And observe, there are not, as the ancient Magi
and the Manicheans taught, two independent
principles, the one of good and the other of evil.
GOD is supreme over every other spirit.   His Will
is absolute.   Nothing can be done in the wide
universe that is not brought under the eye of the
Almighty Ruler.   The eyes of the LORD are in
every place, beholding the evil and the good.
Satan is always represented as in an inferior position, not as contending on an equality with GOD
for the mastery of the world, and dominion over
the souls of men, but acting in subordination to
Him, and performing only such acts as GOD for
His own wise purpose permits.

But far in wonder beyond the records of these

temptations which we have already considered, is that marvellous narrative, the temptation by the Devil in person of our LORD JESUS CHRIST. How Satan could have dared to tempt One so holy; how he could have, for a moment, imagined that he could possibly succeed, appears to us inconceivable. The difficulty is partly answered by the observation of Origen, that though JESUS CHRIST, the SON of GOD, was incapable of sin, yet that Satan did not certainly know Him at that time to be so; he viewed Him only as one of like passions with the rest of human beings, and had not learned to know and to fear Him as the SON of GOD, until his defeated machinations convinced him of the truth.

The temptations with which Satan assailed our LORD exhibit an exact type or representation of those to which mankind are liable.

With regard to these temptations with which Satan assailed our LORD, as well as those which Job resisted, and those under which our first parents fell, there are those, as I have said, who regard them not as actual events, but as allegories and myths; not, indeed, without foundation, but still as not to be taken in their strictly literal sense; and some do not believe them at all. It is one of the special temptations of the devil in the present day that men fancy they have attained 'ch knowledge that they will not believe anything which they cannot understand, at least, in spiritual things. One would have thought that the present state of philosophical and scientific knowledge *ought* to have had exactly the contrary effect, namely, to convince men of their ignorance, rather than their knowledge, for surely if science has taught us anything, it has taught us the narrow limits of our poor capacity when compared with the infinity of God's work. And if the visible and material universe transcends our power of comprehension, how much less are we able to comprehend the mysteries of the invisible world. "Hardly do we guess aright at things that are upon earth, and with labour do we find the things that are before us, but the things that are in heaven who hath searched out ?"[1]

With respect, however, to the special subject of our consideration—the existence of the Devil—the extent of his power, the mode of his operation, and other questions relating to him, there is one consideration which must practically set aside further cavil. It seems to be tacitly assumed by some that if we view the notices in the Bible about the temptation of the Devil, such, I mean, as those which I have mentioned, as figurative only and symbolical ; we do, in some degree, rid ourselves of the apprehension and dread with which the power of so subtle and inveterate an enemy

[1] Wisdom ix. 16.

must fill us. But if we consider the matter we
must acknowledge that what is recorded does but
set before us in vivid character the very facts
which our own daily experience teaches us. We
do in no way mend the matter by regarding
them as myths, because they represent to us facts
and principles to the truth of which our own conscience and experience must bear witness. That
there is an evil personal agent who tempts us to
sin we believe on the authority of God's Word,
but it comes to much the same practically, whether
the Devil is but the symbol of man's corrupt
nature. I do not, for a moment, admit that such
is the case. I only say that the sceptic gains
nothing by denying the personal agency of Satan
in the affairs of men.

We read with admiration Milton's glorious
conception of the war in heaven between the
powers of good and evil—light and darkness.
We know that much of these wondrous pictures
is but the product of the poet's imagination.
We acknowledge the powerlessness of the human
mind to conceive in their details all the accompaniments of this great contest. Still not the less
every consideration shows us that there is a real
conflict going forward in this world between good
and evil, and that the heart of man is the battle-
field on which the contest is fought. Human
science can teach us absolutely nothing on this

deeply spiritual subject. Why not then accept
with faith and reverence the account which Holy
Scripture gives us of the personality of the rivals
who contend for the mastery in this tremendous
strife? Why not avail ourselves with humble
gratitude of the sure salvation offered to us in
the Gospel of CHRIST?

There is one form of temptation which has
sprung up at different times in the world's history,
and is specially rife in the present time—the
temptation to disbelieve GOD's Word—to fancy
that we know better; in a word, the pride of
intellect. When our first mother Eve declared to
the tempter that they were forbidden to eat of the
fruit of the knowledge of good and evil, the tempter
with bold audacity declared, " Ye shall not surely
die, for GOD doth know that in the day ye eat
thereof then your eyes shall be opened, and ye
shall be as GOD, knowing good and evil." Is
not this the very temptation which assails the
philosophers of the present day? They will not
believe GOD's Word—they fancy they know better. They will not believe that GOD will punish
sin—especially the sin of infidelity. And refusing
to believe themselves, they become the agents of
the tempter, and endeavour by wicked devices to
lead others into the same sin and scepticism as
themselves—even as the serpent first tempted Eve
to her destruction, and then made use of her in-

fluence to deceive her husband—so now, he first
tempts weak and sinful men to dare to disbelieve
the Word of God, and then uses their perverted
talents for the destruction of those who are so
imprudent as to listen to their seduction.

If this be allegory, it is not less the truth.

But the simple fact is that the whole matter is
altogether beyond the scope of philosophy. The
philosopher is only making a fool of himself when
he presumes to meddle with such matters. He
knows absolutely nothing from philosophy of
these matters. He must believe the testimony of
God's Word, or reject it at his peril.

There is one other point to which I would
briefly advert. Some might ask, Why does the
Great Ruler of the universe permit Satan to do
all this mischief? Why not destroy him and his
works, and root them out? This was the question asked by the servants of the householder in
that remarkable parable, the parable of the tares.
It may seem at first a paradox to assert that evil
is permitted for the real benefit and perfecting
God's elect. But if there were no physical evil
in the world, no poverty, no disease, no misery,
where would be the field for the exercise of the
self-denying labours of those holy men and
women who devote themselves to labours of love?
Again, temptation is essential to the exercise and
trial of God's servants; and gives occasion to the

development of the highest graces of the Spirit.
How otherwise would they be trained in the
highest of all Christian graces—charity. We
beseech our FATHER in heaven to forgive us our
trespasses as we forgive them that trespass against
us. But if none trespassed against us, if there
were no provocation, no reviling, no injurious
dealing, there would be no opportunity for exercising the Evangelical graces of forgiveness, meekness, gentleness, long-suffering. So if there were
no contradiction of ungodly men, no over-bearing
or tyranny, there would be no occasion for the
exercise of the heavenly virtues of patience and
forbearance. For this end it is, doubtless, that
GOD suffers Satan and his evil agents to tempt
and vex us mortals, in order that by the exercise
of faith and piety, long-suffering and forgiveness,
we may contribute to the glory of GOD, and attain
a brighter resurrection.

This argument does not bear so much on the
question of the origin of evil, as on its continuance—
why, when it had entered into the world, GOD does
not stamp it out—why He does not root out the
tares which the enemy hath sown. The contemplation of the subject will, I think, lead us into
some of the most wondrous depths of Christian
philosophy.

CHAPTER XIX.

REVIVAL OF PAGANISM.—THE CREED OF EPICURUS.—ITS
UTTER SELFISHNESS AND SHORT-SIGHTEDNESS.

IT is generally supposed by not very thoughtful
persons that the world is a good deal wiser than
it used to be,—that the human intellect has
marched on in double quick time in the last century, or half century. Of course as regards mere
material science there is some truth in this
opinion. Except in times of revolution and
anarchy, science must advance, just as in building a house those who build the walls advance on
those who lay the foundation, and those who
crown the edifice with the roof, advance on those
who have built the walls. But the crowners of
the edifice cannot claim any superior wisdom or
knowledge above those who laid the foundation.
The present race of natural philosophers have a
great advantage over those which have gone before them in the improvement of mechanical instruments. If our forefathers had possessed micro-
scopes and telescopes like those in present use,

they might have made as many discoveries as the present men of science,—and without these appliances, it may be doubted whether the present men would have discovered what they have. So that any claim of superior intellect in the present generation would be very doubtful.

However, this is not the matter which I desire to insist on. What I wish now to point out is that though in mere physical science the present generation of philosophers has made a considerable advance, yet that in real philosophy—the philosophy of morals, the knowledge of human life, its relations, duties and tendencies, the philosophers of the present year, 1873, have retrograded from the position even of their fathers, they have in truth gone back in the world's history about 2000 years.

The simple fact is that some of those who profess and call themselves philosophers in the sent age are neither more nor less than Epicureans.

The late Mr. George Grote, the historian, has in his appendix to his book on Aristotle a chapter on Epicurus, a few extracts from which will show the close resemblance between the opinions of some modern philosophers and the sect of Epicureans.

" It was a capital error (Epicurus declared) to suppose that the gods employed themselves as

agents in working or superintending the march
of the kosmos, [the world,] or in conferring
favours on some men, and administering chastisements to others. The vulgar religious tales
which represented them in this manner were untrue and insulting as regards the gods themselves,
and pregnant with perversion and misery as regards the hopes and fears of mankind. . . . .
Epicurus thought that the perfect, eternal, and
unperturbable well-being and felicity of the gods
excluded the supposition of their being agents.
He looked upon them as types of that unmolested
safety, and unalloyed satisfaction, which was
what he understood by pleasure and happiness;
as objects of reverential envy, whose sympathy he
was likely to obtain by assimilating his own temper and conditions to them as far as human circumstances allowed. These theological views were
placed by Epicurus in the foreground of his
ethical philosophy. . . . He disallowed all prophecy, divination, and oracular inspiration, by
which the public around him believed that the
gods were perpetually communicating special revelations to individuals, and for which Socrates
felt so peculiarly thankful." Is not this very
closely allied to the theology of some modern
philosophers ? If they admit that there must
have been a First Cause who made the world,
they deny that He takes any care of His creatures.

They refuse to acknowledge Him as a Father, much more as a Saviour. They imagine that He listens to no prayer, gives no communication of His laws, in short, that He takes no interest whatever in the creatures which He has made. The Christian views GOD as a GOD of love, a FATHER Who careth for His children, and above all things desires their happiness. The wonderful love of GOD the SON in the redemption of the world, our modern philosophers utterly ignore.

"The physics of Epicurus was borrowed in the main from the atomic theory of Democritus, but modified by him in a manner subservient and contributory to his ethical scheme. To that scheme it was essential that those celestial, atmospheric, or terrestrial phenomena which the public around him ascribed to the agency and purposes of the gods, should be understood as being produced by physical causes." He denied, like our modern philosophers, that GOD ever interposed in the works and laws of creation. In fact, if he believed in any God at all, he carefully excluded him from all concern or care for the work of his hands.

The moral views of the Epicureans agree with this notion about their gods. "The standard of virtue and vice is referred by Epicurus to pleasure and pain. Pain is the only evil, pleasure is the only good. Virtue is no end in itself to be sought, vice is no end in itself to be avoided. The motive for cultivating virtue and banishing vice arises from the consequences of each as the means of multiplying pleasures and averting and lessening pains. But to the attainment of this purpose the complete supremacy of reason is indispensable; in order that we may take a right comparative measure of the varieties of pleasure and pain, and pursue the course which promises the least amount of suffering." It is fair to add that he considered the mental element to outweigh the mere body both in pleasure and pain; as no doubt modern philosophers,—say at a meeting of the British Association,—consider the eclât of their scientific lectures to outweigh the pleasures of the good fare which follows them.

Amongst the chief evils of this life Epicurus considered to be the "two greatest torments of human existence—the fear of death, and of eternal suffering after death, as announced by prophets and poets, and the fear of the gods." In fact, Epicurus did not believe in the continued existence of the soul. He supposed that a man might live a luxurious, self-indulgent life,—gratify all his worst propensities of lust and cruelty, tyrannize over his fellow-creatures, and yet die in a good old age without fear of future accountability. Is not this the very same feeling which in the present day impels men to deny the eternity of punishment, and reject the warnings of the Athanasian Creed? But *can* men who live in a Christian age *really* put from them the dreadful feeling that in spite of their wilful scepticism these things may be true? The Epicurean notion of escaping the punishment of evil deeds after death can scarcely be attained by those who have heard GOD's Revelation. The worst of men have been most haunted by superstitious terrors. How much wiser, how much more philosophical in every way to accept the mercy of GOD, and lead holy lives.

Human happiness consisted, according to Epicurus, "in the satisfaction of the wants of life, and the conversation of friends . . . . a tranquil, undisturbed, innocuous, non-competitive fruition which approached most nearly to the perfect happiness of the gods"—no fear of future punishment—no hope of future recompense for the righteous.

It is not difficult to understand why such persons as the Sadducees amongst the Jews, and the Epicureans amongst the Greek and Romans, and others like them, in every age of the world should have held sceptical opinions respecting a future state of existence. Enjoying in this world all the gratifications which wealth and power could afford, dazzled by worldly vanities, immersed in the turmoil of business, or sunk in sensual in-

P

dulgence, they felt how utterly unfitted they were
for pure and spiritual enjoyments : and so, because they were conscious that, if a day of retribution should arrive, it would be to them a day
of sorrow and confusion, they resolved to banish
the subject from their minds. Because they had
nothing to hope they resolved if possible to fear
nothing. They vainly thought to make a com-
promise between heaven and hell by persuading
themselves to disbelieve the existence of either.
They imagined that they could escape the danger
by closing their eyes against it, as the foolish
ostrich fancies that he can escape his pursuers by
plunging his head into the sand. They forgot
that their opinion could have no possible influence
one way or the other, but that the rewards and
punishments of another world would be just as
real and true whether they chose to believe them
or not.

And did it never occur to these philosophers
that it is most unreasonable to judge of the pros-
pects of the whole human race, by the present
condition of a small part of them ? It may be
that they themselves enjoyed their present existence, and, on condition that they might be
allowed free scope for the indulgence of their ease
and carnal pursuits, would ignobly barter their
hopes of life eternal. And they felt doubtless that to deny the doctrine of future retribu-

tion was to remove a thorn from their side, and take away the bitterest ingredient from their cup of worldly pleasure. But, with characteristic selfishness, they forgot the case of hundreds of thousands and millions of human beings, to whom this life is one unbroken series of hardship and toil.

Could Epicurus and his friends—can modern philosophers whose creed agrees with his—for a moment look on the state of the world around them and imagine that this is the whole of man's existence? If "this tranquil, undisturbed, innocuous, non-competitive fruition, and satisfaction of the wants of life" is the *summum bonum* of human existence, does it not occur to them that the vast majority of the human race ·are hopelessly debarred from ever attaining happiness of this sort? Almighty GOD, or Fate, as the philosophers would say, has imposed on all but a few a continual struggle for existence; they are doomed to eat bread in the sweat of their brow. Can it for a moment be believed that nothing is in store after this life for the honest and laborious sons of toil who pass through this world in performing the duties of the station to which GOD has called them? Is this poor life with all its labour, and disappointment, pain, and inevitable disease, all that GOD has prepared for those who serve Him faithfully?

Yet so it is supposed by these philosophers.
While God's minister holds out the happiness
of heaven as the sure reward of all those who
serve God faithfully in this life, the heartless
scepticism of the philosopher would lead to the
conclusion, that the destiny of poor suffering
mortals after the miseries of this sinful world
is either to be for ever miserable, or for ever—
nothing; that is, simply annihilation or hell!

For men who have once heard the blessed
tidings of the Gospel to go back to the dreary
creed of Epicurus, and bring themselves to believe
that this life is the whole of their existence, that
no punishment is in store for the wicked, no
reward for those who diligently seek the Lord, is
a proof, if none other were assignable, that the
human intellect is not so progressive as modern
philosophers would persuade us. But as Mr.
Grote says, "It is certain that he [Epicurus]
disregarded the logical part of the process, the
systematic study of propositions, and their relations of consistency one with another"—in all
this how exactly in accordance with the theories
of modern philosophers.

It would be unjust not to mention that the
Epicureans spoke highly of justice and friendship.
They considered that just and righteous dealing
was the indispensable condition to every one's
comfort, because if a man was unjust to others he
could not expect others to be just to him.   They

insisted also on the value of friendship as a means of happiness to both the persons so united. Yes, "the greatest happiness principle" is no invention of modern philosophers, but simply a going back to Pagan precedents. I have no doubt that our modern sceptics are men of strict justice—they pay their just debts, because they know the consequences if they do not—and will ask their friends to dinner, not without the hope of a similar entertainment in return. And yet these very men are they who, by the dogmas which they promulgate, are ruining the souls of thousands of their fellow-creatures, in utter carelessness of the destruction which they are scattering.

I am afraid that I shall be guilty of a bathos in suggesting one argument which modern Epicureans perhaps have overlooked. If there are no rewards and punishments in the world to come, it is surely unfair that some people should have so much of this world's goods, and others so little. If, indeed, the poverty of Lazarus in this life is to be made up to him at the feast of heaven, he may well endure his worldly privation with patience. But if there is to be no such rectification of this world's anomalies, and no punishment for robbery and violence, what is to prevent the Communist from taking measures to equalize the present condition of men, and force his rich neighbour to share with him his worldly goods? This seems to be a just corollary of the doctrine of Epicurus.

CHAPTER XX.

THERE are different degrees of wrong-headedness amongst those who refuse to walk in wisdom's way. "How long," says the wise man, "how long, ye simple ones, will ye love simplicity, and the scorners delight in their scorning, and fools hate knowledge?" Three sorts of persons are here addressed. First, "simple ones." The simple ones are those who are not presumptuously wicked, but are led astray from true religion by trifling and unworthy objects. Like children, they seem not to appreciate the consequences of their actions. A child, or schoolboy, does not discern the advantage of the instruction and discipline to which he is subject. He does not understand how necessary it is for his welfare in after life to be able to read and write, to learn Latin and Greek, mathematics, and modern languages. He loves his sports and pastimes—his tops and marbles, his cricket and boating, and grudges if they be interfered with. He would gladly throw his books into the fire, and spend all his time in amusement. Just so the simple ones amongst grown-up men and women are wont to be wholly taken up with their present enjoyments and occupations. They dance and sing, and adorn themselves, and occupy their time in these various pleasures, recreations, flirtations—or, even in the case of grave men, they are so full of their favourite pursuits, their politics and business, their speculations and schemes of getting rich, and rising in the world—or with pursuits more doubtful even than these—their sporting and horse-racing, pigeon-shooting, their mountain-climbing and yachting; or, if they are philosophers, they are so eager about their experiments and researches, calculations and investigations, and articles in reviews—many of them, no doubt, excellent things in their way—that they fancy they have no time for the concerns of eternity. Grave matters of religion seem to them of far inferior moment to their favourite pursuits, and this not so much from absolute wickedness as from simplicity or frivolousness, or mere incapacity to discern the relative value of things. And as children will often bestow ten times as much pains on some comparatively worthless labour of their own choosing, as on that which their parents or teachers set them to do, so the simple ones of the

world, immersed in mere temporal pursuits, worn
out with toil for that which perisheth in the
gaining, labouring for bread which satisfieth not,
fancying that they are bestowing their pains on
some vastly important object, do in the meantime
overlook that which is the real business of life,
neglect to acquaint themselves with GOD, and live
to His glory, and improve the grace given them,
and cultivate those holier faculties which may fit
them for a higher state of existence.   The sacred
labour of self-discipline, subduing evil within
them, communing with GOD and the spiritual
world, exercising themselves in prayer and holy
meditation—all this appears to them irksome and
unprofitable, and so they put it away.   They
hope, it may be, to attend to religion some day,
but the years speed on, and, too often, find the
simple ones still engaged in their vanities, still
loving their simplicity.

The next class of irreligious persons is worse
than that already described—inasmuch as there is
more of wilfulness and deliberation in their irreligion.   The simple are irreligious from thoughtlessness, but scorners are men who of set purpose,
and from a sort of strange pleasure, "delight in
their scorning."   There are too many of this sort
in the world around us.   The unbridled liberty of
thought and speech in which men of the present
age so much boast themselves, has led many to

scorn and despise religion, and scoff at all that is good, and excellent, and holy. The root of evil in them is pride—pride of intellect—conceit of their own ability. It is not that, like the former class, they are led astray by thoughtlessness and simplicity, but they scorn holy things and holy men—look down upon them, laugh at what is good.

But there is a worse class of men than even these; "fools that hate knowledge"—not only scorn, but hate it. It is not mere thoughtlessness, or self-conceit that characterizes the irreligion of these men—but positive hatred of what is good and holy. The wise man speaks in very strong terms of the wickedness of such as these. "The fool hath said in his heart, There is no GOD." "Fools make a mock at sin." "Foolish men blaspheme GOD." "Fools despise wisdom and instruction." "The fool rageth, and is confident." "Though thou shouldst bray a fool in a mortar, yet will his foolishness not depart from him." From which various descriptions of the character of the fool, it appears that it is not mere deficiency of judgment and knowledge; but there is in him a sort of wilful obstinacy and wrongheadedness, which causes him to harden his heart against true wisdom, and continue resolutely in his sin and error. It is astonishing with what determination men of this sort set themselves against religion, what futile and shallow arguments they often use; at other times, with what ingenuity they frame excuses for continuing in their evil headstrong course. For these men are commonly no fools in worldly matters, but shrewd enough in temporal things, clever it may be in mere material philosophy—only fools, desperate fools, in things which concern the good of their souls. Hence it is that they " hate knowledge." Real knowledge—that is, knowledge of GOD's Truth, reminds the fool of his danger, checks him in the midst of his folly, sets before him his real condition, shows him that however wise he may be in the world's wisdom, yet if he loses his soul he will be obliged to confess one day " that he has played the fool, and erred exceedingly." But these things the fool does not like to be reminded of. And because GOD's Word reminds him of them he hates it ; and if at any time he hears GOD's ministers say anything which reminds him of his folly, he hates them too. " Hast thou found me, O mine enemy ?" said Ahab to Elijah. Thus the fool thinks GOD's ministers his enemies. No one is louder against priestcraft, and bigotry, and superstition, than the man of this character. Even if he is brought to acknowledge his sinfulness and the need of repentance, he hardens his heart against the means whereby pardon may be sought and obtained. Self-discipline, self-

examination, secret communing with GOD, holy
ordinances, sacraments, confession of sin—all
these are his special aversion. Hence it is that
the fool is in so hopeless a case—there is no
getting at his heart to do him good. For even if
he knows his disease, he is too proud and obstinate to adopt the means necessary for his recovery.
He has an inveterate distaste for all that is lowly,
humbling, self-denying—all that is pure, holy,
and religious—he hates knowledge, and will have
none of its counsel. This sort of wilful dogged
sin, is closely allied to the sin against the HOLY
GHOST, which can be forgiven neither in this
world nor in the world to come, because it consists in putting from us wilfully and angrily the
remedy by which our disease might be cured.
And a man who has brought himself to this state
of mind becomes the instrument of Satan for the
destruction of others. Not content with ruining
their own souls, men of this sort have a strange
and fiendish delight in beguiling others to their
ruin, spreading around evil opinions, alluring men
to unbelief, contempt of Scripture, neglect of holy
things—nay, often in deliberately seducing them
into bad, immoral habits—so closely connected is
unbelief and hardness of heart with the most cruel
and degraded vice.

I do not venture to judge individuals, but I
would put it to any one capable of reasoning,

whether it is possible to conceive a more miserable and guilty man than one who of set purpose destroys the soul of his brother—perhaps thousands of his brethren, by undermining their faith in CHRIST. To do so carelessly, or presumptuously, or ignorantly from neglect to ascertain the truth, is a tremendous responsibility; but wilfully to draw souls away from CHRIST, is nothing short of the malice of the Arch-Fiend himself.

I must not conclude these bitter, but most true, words of remonstrance without adding from the same page of Scripture some which are more hopeful and consolatory. "Turn ye," says the wise man, "turn ye at my reproof, and I will pour out my spirit unto you, and I will make known my words unto you:" "If thou wilt incline thine ear unto wisdom, and apply thy heart to understanding—yea, if thou criest after knowledge, and liftest up thy voice for understanding; if thou seekest her as silver, and searchest for her as hid treasure, then shalt thou understand the fear of the LORD and find the knowledge of GOD. . . . . Happy is the man that findeth wisdom, and the man that getteth understanding ; for the merchandise of it is better than the merchandise of silver, and the gain thereof than fine gold. . . . Length of days is in her right hand, and in her left hand riches and honour. Her ways are ways of pleasantness, and all her paths are peace."

CHAPTER XXI.

EFFECTS OF ATHEISM.—"A RETROGRADATION TO SAVAGERY."

THERE seems to be an infatuated blindness in the public mind, even amongst religious people, with regard to the tendency of the philosophical scepticism of the present day. It is not that warning voices are not uttered, but people do not attend to them. They seem to think that things will go on very comfortably, that we shall continue as we are, a rich and peaceful community, that our prosperity will remain as yesterday, and even more abundant. They are blind, or rather shut their eyes, to the fact that many serious evils are growing up, that good old principles are wearing out, new and dangerous feelings pervading the public mind, old-fashioned notions of religion and obedience to law are becoming sadly obliterated.

In particular the tremendous example of France in the last century is gradually wearing out in the minds of Englishmen. In our younger days

the example of the French Revolution was held
up as a warning against Atheism and insubordi-
nation. No one doubted, and none doubt even
now, if they do but think of it, that the almost
unparalleled sufferings of France at the end of the
last century, and not yet brought to a termination, sprang from the Atheism which had been
imbibed from the writings of the Encyclopædists,
and sceptical philosophers, Voltaire, Rousseau,
Diderot, and others, who corrupted the public
mind. Nor was it less doubted that the ex-
emption of England from the same horrors of
revolution was due to the maintenance of our
principles of religion and public order. But these
wholesome impressions seem to have died away.
Religion has come to be thought an affair between each man and GOD alone. Sceptical philosophers spread the most pestiferous doctrines
broad-cast through the land, and unthinking
people encourage, or at least listen with interest to,
their unwholesome speculations. Sceptical literature obtains abundant circulation, from some of
the articles in the *Contemporary* down to *Reynolds'*,
or the mock Litanies, in many of which Atheism
is mingled with the most atrocious and murderous
principles. Let any one, if he wishes to satisfy
himself on this head, just go through a course of
Reynolds' for a few weeks. I myself have done
so. The very first paragraph which caught my

eye was to the following effect : " If all the kings
and princes of Europe were placed in a row, and
a mitrailleuse pointed at them, who that valued
the interests of humanity would not say—fire ?"
These notions of mixed Atheism and Revolution
spread themselves gradually, or rather rapidly,
through all classes.   Our villages are not free
from the contagion.   A half drunken man reels
out from a debate in the beer-shop, with the
words, " Well, all that I can say is, that all rich
people ought to be hanged."   And so I have no
doubt a good many will be hanged, if the people
are made Atheists. Such are the sort of words
which one may hear even in a rural village ; judge
what may be heard amongst the roughs in our
great towns.   There cannot be the slightest doubt,
that the combined influence of Infidelity and Revolution is widely spreading throughout the land,
and threatens a subversion of our political and
social institutions.

It will be said, perhaps, that circumstances
differ very much in this country from those which
existed in France before the French Revolution.
Of course they do; you might point out many
things quite different, but I fear many are essentially the same.   It may be said that there is not
in this country the same marked distinction between classes, the *noblesse* on the one hand, the
canaille on the other.   There is a great middle

class which holds the scales between them.   Yes,
but there has grown up in England a demarcation
of classes which is equally dangerous, in some respects more so.   The division which exists between labour and capital separates the community
into two antagonistic parties.   It may be quite
right—I believe it is so—that workmen's and la-
bourers' wages should be raised in proportion to
the rise in articles of consumption.   We may
hope that things may yet right themselves: still
there is manifest danger ahead.   What is the
cause of the wealth and prosperity of England?
What but the industry and skill of her people.
But if the English workman will not work, if he
does less work than the men of other countries,
the very source of our wealth is cut off.   At present we have to import nearly one half of the food
we consume, and pay for it by the manufactures
which we send out.   But if the people will not
work, and consequently are not able to send out
manufactures in payment for their food, there is
no help for it but that there will be a general
scramble for what is left.   This year we happen
to be in the full flood of prosperous commerce.
Next year or the year after there may be a reaction.   Then will come the trial.   It will be absolutely impossible for the employers of labour to
pay the same wages as they are now paying for a
reduced amount of work.   What will our work-

men do for their beer and other indulgences, not
to speak of the maintenance of their families?
They are, I fear, as a body utterly unable to understand the position of affairs. Their ears will
be open only to the counsel of demagogues. Will
the country stand the pressure? If all classes
were embued with the spirit of Christianity there
might be a better hope. Patient endurance on the
part of the poor, self-denying charity on the part
of the rich, might, by GOD's blessing, bring us
through. But, alas! Christian principle has been
undermined by the philosophers. It is well if
society is not resolved into its elements, and an
universal scramble takes place for the mere neces-
saries of existence. Communists and Socialists
will avail themselves of the opportunity to upset
all that remains of social order and religion, and
England may present a spectacle of misfortune,
such as the world has not before witnessed.

Most people who think at all about such subjects, deem it at least possible that some such
state of things awaits us. Some, of course, are
more sanguine. They think if there was a row
in London, for instance, that all the better sort of
people would unite together as they did in 1848
—that we should have 200,000 special constables
prepared to put down riot and revolution. GOD
grant it may be so! But, first, we have not the
Duke of Wellington to organize our defence;

Q

again, I question whether there is the same spirit
amongst our better class of people, or the same
energy in our rulers. We must remember the
day of the Park palings. Some will say, it can
never be in London as it was lately in Paris, when
the Communists were drilled, and had 300 can-
nons, and an unlimited supply of arms. Well,
but there may be some other concatenation of circumstances equally dangerous. One of our greatest misfortunes is the want of principle in political
parties. It may suit the leader of a party—or he
may fancy it will suit him—to let his friends, the
mob, have their way for a while, and all Government may be toppled over before we are aware
of it.

But, not if there were a good religious spirit in
the people. If we were a nation of Christians,
who believed in the great doctrines of religion,
and were trained to regard them; if men, both
rich and poor, acted under the constant impression
that there was a heaven and hell, and an account
to be given at the last day, a GOD the FATHER
Who rules us, a SAVIOUR Who has redeemed us,
and a HOLY GHOST Who would enable us to lead
godly lives, of course, there would be no danger
of a violent and murderous revolution. But our
sceptical philosophers have done what they can to
undermine all these principles, though, thank
GOD, there are many good Christians amongst us,

prepared to do and to suffer; yet, thanks to the philosopher, a spirit of unbelief has spread throughout the masses, and we can no longer trust for safety to the right feeling of our people.

Amongst the minor evil effects of the recent tendency to scepticism is the following, which I find in the pages of the *Contemporary Review*, (Sep. 1873, p. 572) :—" The insolent discourtesy towards ladies, exhibited, not here and there, but at almost every recent gathering of the upper classes. . . . . In ceasing to be Christians they have ceased to be gentlemen." A most natural consequence, and much to be deplored.

Of course, the principal evil, which arises from the un-Christianizing of the nation, by our philosophical sceptics, is the fearful loss of souls, which must infallibly happen. Still, it is not necessary for the Christian to leave altogether out of the question the temporal ruin which will be entailed by the prevalence of the same principle. Imagine, for a moment, that the Atheists had their way—that they persuaded the people generally that there was no Judgment, no account to be given after this World—no Heaven and Hell. Imagine the mass of our people to become under such teaching a horde of Atheists—unbelievers in a GOD and SAVIOUR, acting on the principle, "Let us eat and drink, for to-morrow we die." Instead of hearing, as they now do week by week from the pulpit, exhortations to serve GOD, and love their neighbour, and lead good and honest lives, and if they have sinned, to repent and turn to GOD, and keep His Commandments for the future, suppose that philosophic infidels persuaded the people to adopt their principles,—what a wild scene of reckless havoc and confusion would ensue! An age of darkness might be expected to arise, far more gloomy and disastrous than any that the world has seen. To describe the misery of living in such a period of the world is impossible—the scenes of horror and confusion which would certainly arise if religion were banished from our land can be imagined, but not depicted. There would be, as it has been well expressed, "a retrogradation to savagery." Are there not some men even now—some who have figured in recent scenes in other countries— who are worse than gorillas?

Yet it is the avowed object of some of our leading philosophers to destroy the Faith of CHRIST from the land!

CHAPTER XXII

WHAT a strange, illiberal, bigoted notion it is in
the estimation of the advanced Liberals and men
of the world, that we ought to make any difference in our behaviour to people on account of
their religious belief! What! not receive a man
into your house who does not abide in the true
doctrine of CHRIST, (see 2 S. John 9,) not bid
him GOD speed if he happens not to agree with
you in your religious views? Why this is more
fit for the days of the Inquisition, or of the Star
Chamber, than for the nineteenth century! and
yet these are the very words of the Disciple whom
JESUS loved,—the most loving and affectionate of
all the Disciples. And they agree entirely with
the words of the other Apostles, nay, of our LORD
Himself,—" Now, I beseech you, mark them that
cause divisions and offences contrary to the doctrine which ye have received, and avoid them."
" In the last days perilous times shall come, for

men shall be lovers of their own selves, ...
heady, high-minded, ... having the form of
godliness, but denying the power thereof : from
such turn away." It is clear that the lax and
liberal notions of the present day on these matters are clean contrary to the letter and spirit of
the ever blessed Gospel. So much the worse for
the Gospel, the infidel would say. But I am
addressing Christians, and endeavouring to show
what line of conduct their religion requires of
them.

I cannot believe that those who think and
speak lightly of atheism and unbelief are the
most charitable. They may really be doing the
unbelievers the greatest injury which one man
can do to another, by making them disregard the
sin of unbelief, and so confirming them in their
unhappy course. In fact it is just the eclat bestowed on clever sceptics which is the moving
cause of their scepticism, or at least of their endeavours to give it notoriety.

You will hear unthinking persons refer to the
example of the Good Samaritan. Here, say they,
is an example of real charity. The Good Samaritan never thought of inquiring what religion
the wounded traveller was of,—whether he was
his fellow-countryman, or one of the hostile race
of Judea; but as soon as he saw his miserable
plight, he went at once and raised him from the

ground, and bound up his wounds and conveyed
him to a place of safety.   Yes; and I hope every
true Christian would go and do likewise.   If we
saw a stranger lying on the roadside in affliction,
and suffering, who would ever think of inquiring
what religion he was of before rendering him
assistance?   The idea is absurd.   We should regard him simply as a fellow-creature who was in
need of present assistance, and promptly render
him all the help we could.   And yet I see nothing absurd in the habit of good George Herbert,
who, when a beggar asked for alms, would require
him to say the Creed and the LORD's Prayer, and
if he found him able to repeat them, would relieve
him the more liberally..   It would rather surprise
some of our tramps in the present day, if, when
they begged of the parson of the parish, he made
them say their Catechism.   Yet they would have
no reason to complain if they got another six-
pence, or perhaps a good meal for their proficiency.
Certainly George Herbert's plan was quaint, like
his poems, yet it involves the true principle that
we ought to " do good unto all men, and specially
to those that are of the household of faith."

I am reminded of another story which was
told, I think, of the celebrated Wesley, illustrative of the duty of avoiding the irreligious.   Once
on a time in his journeyings he was benighted
and overtaken by a violent storm, and was glad

to take shelter in a comfortable farmhouse, where he was hospitably received, and a night's lodging freely offered him. Before retiring to rest, he looked for the assembly of the members of the family for prayer, and greatly was he surprised when he found that such was not their intention,—though he himself offered to officiate, they refused to accept his service.   But his resolution was at once taken. He went forth and saddled his horse, and pursued his journey, preferring to brave the discomforts of the pelting storm, rather than pass the night under a roof where no prayer was offered for God's mercy, no thanksgiving for His goodness.

These may appear to some overstrained sentiments, but the stories well illustrate the duty of regarding the religious character of those with whom we associate in contradistinction to the lax morality of those who view the Christian and the infidel with the same regard.

It is far too much the practice in the present day to think and speak lightly of such transgressions as do not interfere with our own personal comfort and safety. We are ready enough to bring the strong arm of the law to bear on those who are guilty of crimes from which we apprehend that we ourselves may suffer in our persons or our property ; there is great indignation against thieves, murderers, housebreakers, impostors, cheats, and little pity is felt for such persons when detected and punished. But there are also many criminals equally culpable in the sight of GOD whose sins are commonly palliated from a feeling of spurious charity. Drunkards are spoken of as no man's enemies but their own; heretics and unbelievers are regarded as justified in holding what opinions they please; and the fact of their corrupting GOD's truth, destroying men's souls, is looked upon as an affair in which they themselves only are concerned, and of which no one has any right to complain. There is a common saying which has the semblance of Christian sentiment, but as commonly applied, is a mere maxim of latitudinarianism, that "we ought to hate the sin, but love the sinner." If by "loving the sinner" is meant that we ought to pity and pray for him, and endeavour to redeem him from his error, the sentiment is just; but if it be meant, as it is too commonly applied, that we ought to behave to the unbeliever and heretic with the same cordiality and respect, and receive him with the same love and affection as we do our Christian brother, then the saying is mischievous and fallacious, and a proof of the irreligious mind of him who utters it.

Think only of the utter difference of principle in the Christian and the unbeliever. The Christian is persuaded that the eternal welfare of souls depends on their accepting the salvation pur-

chased for them by CHRIST. The infidel not
only disbelieves this doctrine, but often does
all in his power to persuade others not to accept
the salvation through CHRIST, and, as we believe,
is the means of ruining the souls of many.   The
Christian believes that righteousness exalteth a
nation, that the prosperity of his country depends
on their being true worshippers of GOD; that if
the nation should reject Christianity, ruin and
misery would fall upon it.   He sees recent evidence of the fearful evil of infidel opinions in the
horrible anarchy which quite recently afflicted
France during the rule of the Communists, which
was greatly surpassed at the time of the first
French Revolution.   Spain is even at the present
moment exhibiting an example of the tremendous
evil of ungodliness.   How can a man who views
things in this light feel friendship for those who
are actively encouraging principles which have
worked so much misery?

Again, the Christian believes that the only safe
mode of bringing up the rising generation in
good and honest ways, is by educating them from
their earliest infancy in the true doctrines of
CHRIST.   In that faith he brings up his own
children, and desires to see those of his fellow-
subjects brought up, deeming that it would be
the greatest boon the nation could confer upon
them.   But there are men who do all they can to

frustrate the religious education of the people,—
who obstruct by every means in their power this
communication of religious knowledge, religious
habits, and principle, and impede the endeavours
of good men to imbue the youthful mind of the
nation with the principles of CHRIST's true religion. How can Christian men have any sympathy or fellowship with men who act on principles such as these; who, not content themselves
to live without GOD in this world, perversely do
all in their power to thwart the labours of
GOD's servants to spread the knowledge of the
truth ?

I have in a former chapter adverted to the
most cruel and audacious attempt to undervalue
the duty and privilege of prayer. Alas! how
much have they to answer for who have prejudiced
the minds of any against this chief instrument of
godliness and salvation, and, it may be, prevented
the poor helpless sinner from availing himself of
what might have softened his hard heart, and
brought him in true penitence to GOD's foot-
stool.

The question is, if question there can be, what
should be the conduct and bearing of Christians
towards men like these who oppose and frustrate
what we hold to be most vital and holy. There
can be no doubt that it is the duty of those who
love GOD to set their faces with a righteous indig-

nation against GOD's enemies, the breakers of
GOD's commandments, the blasphemers of His
Name, and all who in any way resist His authority, corrupt His Word, and deny the faith.
Against such as. these it is our bounden duty to
be ready at all times to protest with all our might,
and to take heed that we give them no countenance or encouragement, lest we be partakers of
their evil deeds, and sharers in their just punishment. And especially those who are placed in
authority,—sovereigns, legislators, magistrates,
masters of families, parents,—all of us, in short,
in our several stations are bound to use the
authority and influence which GOD has given us
for the suppression of vice, and the maintenance
of true religion and virtue.

The following case occurred lately.

At the recent meeting of the British Association
one person said that some part of the human
body, [the vermiform appendage known as the
diverticulum of the cæcum,] " was not an evidence
of Almighty Power, but to be regarded as the
effort of a tinker to mend the error of his works."
And this person was not turned out of the
assembly, nor even called to order! Surely
this was an unworthy carelessness of GOD's
honour.

It will be said, perhaps, that parties, both
religious and political, are so mixed up together—

society is constituted of so many various elements
—that it is impossible to draw a strict line between believers and unbelievers, or to conform
literally to the Apostolic ordinance. Admitting
that there is some show of reason in these objec-
tions, nevertheless it is certain that many things
are done, and done quite unnecessarily, and done
by professing Christians, which seem almost ex-
pressly intended to put aside the Christian duty
which we are considering, and prominently to set
forth the opinion that Christians and infidels
should be placed on the same footing. It does
seem a gratuitous departure from propriety that
men should be buried with all the highest honours
of Christian sepulture amongst the benefactors of
their country, who have habitually kept during
life from within the walls of GOD's house. It
does seem most inconsistent with the character of
politicians, believed to be supporters of GOD's
Church, to come forward to do honour to a man
whose whole life has been spent in counteracting
the doctrine of CHRIST. What are we to say to
the strange anomaly of the University admitting
to its highest honours a man whose most recent
feat has been to dissuade men from the use of
prayer?

I know very well what a sceptic would say in
answer to what I have just written. "Oh, this is
all odium theologicum," he will say. But if this

be "odium theologicum," it only shows that odium theologicum is not so bad a thing as it has been represented. If what they call "odium theologicum" be a just and honest indignation against those who lead their brethren to reject the Gospel of CHRIST, I should say it was an essential part of the Christian character.

CHAPTER XXIII.

THE disputes about education arise principally from not defining what education really is. When different persons, or two different parties, speak of education, they mean quite different things. Let us endeavour to analyse the subject.

All will agree that reading, writing, and arithmetic, are primary requisites for education, and are the necessary-foundations for future acquirements. The boys and girls, brought up at our day-schools, ought, when they leave school at twelve or thirteen, to be able to read fluently, write correctly and grammatically, and know so much of the first rules of arithmetic as may suffice for the requirements of ordinary life. So far all persons are agreed.

But now many people in the present day think that children ought to be scientifically educated. Well. But it is not considered how much of the elementary and most important parts of science come naturally. An infant first opening his eyes knows nothing of optics or perspective. He squints most awfully; one eye looks one way and one another. But nature soon teaches him to adjust the focus and look straight. Again, he sees all things at first as on one plane. He tries to lay hold on the moon, fancying that it is close to him; it is only gradually that he learns the relative distance of objects. Children soon learn the scientific fact that fire will burn their fingers, and observe, with Newton, that apples fall to the ground. An interesting experiment is often made by the young philosopher shying sticks up at the apples, which clearly demonstrates their gravitation to the earth. And this often leads to another discovery in science, namely, that a smart blow on the back from a cane or ash plant so affects the afferent nerve-trunk as to cause considerable pain, and draw tears from the eyes, as Mr. Darwin has so luminously explained. Proceeding on with their scientific education, boys learn that a marble shot with force communicates its force to another marble, on which it impinges, and drives it from the ring, so that it may be lawfully transferred to the pocket. The top, they observe, not only revolves on its own axis, but also forms an orbit round an imaginary centre. A clever master might utilize these experiences, by giving instruction on the revolution of the heavenly bodies, the theory of gravitation and force,

the nature of the nerves, and cerebrum, and many
other useful matters. It is desirable that books
used in schools for instruction in reading should
contain information on common things—inform
the children that the earth goes round the sun,
and not the sun round the earth; what is the
cause of the change from day to night; why the
moon sometimes appears full and sometimes as a
crescent. I think a good deal of this sort of
knowledge might be imparted incidentally—as,
again, why it is that by digging a well you generally come to water; why coal has been called
"bottled sunbeams;" what is the difference between veins and arteries, nerves and muscles, and
a host of things all in a general way; but as to
giving the children of our elementary schools any
systematic knowledge of these things, the time
does not allow of it.

Nor, in fact, would such knowledge be of much
use to them, except in connection with their special occupations. Take one of the most valuable
discoveries of modern times, the steam engine.
Look at the scores of people waiting at the station
to meet the train. How many of these persons
are acquainted with the theory of latent heat, or
even with the structure of the engine which is to
whirl them along—the piston, the crank, the
governor? Very few indeed. What most concerns us all to know is, when the train starts, and

R

when it will take us to our journey's end, and how much we have to pay. The scientific theory and construction of the steam engine are of small importance, except to those who have to make the engine, or to guide it. And so it is in other departments of knowledge. It is very desirable to have a good chemist, and a good lawyer in every town. But it is not necessary to other people to know much about chemistry, and we all know the old saying about the man who is his own lawyer. But while we want only one good chemist, and one lawyer, and one doctor, and one post-master, we want all to be good Christians.

I argue, therefore, that if we send our children from our schools well up in reading, writing, and arithmetic, it is of small importance for them to know much about science; in fact, they have no time to enter, except quite superficially, into the subject.

And it is much the same in the higher departments of education. I am far from saying that it is not desirable for our young men at the universities to know the principles of science. And for this purpose, I would strongly advise them to attend the lectures on geology, anatomy, chemistry, or botany, for all which opportunity is afforded. "This," says Dr. Newman, in his *Grammar of Assent,* " is what is called with special appositeness, a gentleman's knowledge as contrasted with that of a professional man, and is neither worthless nor despicable." But on no account let these pursuits be allowed to displace the old established university studies. It is not necessary for English gentlemen to be chemists, or geologists, or anatomists, beyond knowing the general principle of these sciences. But it *is* necessary for every well-educated man to be acquainted with the literature of past ages—the poets, the orators, the historians of ancient Greece and Rome. In point of fact language is the highest of all sciences; and command of language is of all things most necessary for those who would excel in the senate, the bar, or the pulpit, or exercise important influence for good in any department of life.

But now comes the important question—Is what I have described education? Suppose a boy passes through our elementary schools, and goes home able to read perfectly, to write correctly, and cipher accurately, but is untrained in moral conduct—is untruthful, deceitful, violent, quarrelsome, selfish, "incontinent, fierce, heady, highminded," given to swearing, lying, and bad language, should we say that such a boy was educated? Would any parent think that his son had received a good education? I think not. He would say that he had been shamefully neg-

lected. Was it not the Duke of Wellington who
said that such a system would only train up a set
of " clever devils ?" Surely we ought to educate
the higher nature of youth—train up our children
to be truthful, honest, conscientious, obedient to
law, respectful to authority, resolved always to do
the thing which is right. And not only should
they be trained in the knowledge and practice of
their duty to their fellow-men, but also in the
knowledge of GOD and of all that He requires of
them for their soul's everlasting peace. Give
them all the knowledge you can, but if you neglect their moral character you have done absolutely nothing for their real happiness either in
this world or the world to come.

And if convinced of this important truth, we
come to inquire what means or appliances, what
help or authority the teacher has in this, the highest part of education, we at once should say the
Bible was the instrument given for that very purpose—" How shall a young man cleanse his way?
even by ruling himself after Thy Word." " Evil
men and seducers shall wax worse and worse,
deceiving and being deceived. But continue
thou in the things which thou hast learned, and
hast been assured of, knowing of Whom thou hast
learned them; and that from a child thou hast
known the Holy Scripture, which is able to make
thee wise unto Salvation." The Bible is the

great store-house of all spiritual knowledge, and
furnishes the rule for all right conduct in life.

But now the Bible is a large Book, or rather a
collection of books : it is difficult to understand—
at least it is difficult to comprehend and systema-
tize its contents so as to gain from it a concise
and available rule of faith or conduct. Children
require to be taught the relation in which they
stand to their GOD and FATHER—GOD the FA-
THER Who made them and all the world, GOD
the SON Who redeemed them, and GOD the HOLY
GHOST Who sanctifieth them. They require to
be taught what are the commandments of GOD,
how they may do their duty to GOD and Man,
what are the means which GOD has given to help
them in doing His Will. And what is this that
we have been describing but the Church Catechism—that form of sound words gathered from
Holy Scripture, and put forth by authority, which
sums up the chief points of Christian faith and
duty, and explains the means which GOD has provided for enabling us to live in His faith and fear
—the Creed, the Commandments, the LORD's
Prayer, and the Sacraments. Let children by all
means be taught to read the Bible, and along with
this let them be instructed in the brief and comprehensive summary of Christian faith and duty
which may help them to understand and to prac-
tise what they read.

Let them be practically taught to regard truth —to exercise gentleness and self-denial, to act on Christian motives, to follow the dictates of conscience. Much of this *ought* to be learned at home from their parents; their pastor and schoolmaster should lead them on in right ways.

Another important part of education is that children should be taught to worship GOD. It may not be that they will understand everything they hear in church. But it is a great point for them to be brought betimes under the sacred roof— to see their parents and those whom they look up to engaged in acts of devotion—to hear the solemn chant and anthem, and the Word of GOD publicly read. Let them be taught the principles of religion as their understanding opens, but the feeling of its reality will be best communicated by accustoming them to join in religious worship.

There are two things connected with this subject which appear to me amongst the most strange and unaccountable which have ever been exhibited in the world's history. One is, that in this nineteenth century, which boasts of its intellectual advancement, and progress in civilization and liberality, there are actually men of some intelligence and influence who deliberately desire to separate secular from religious education, who propose to bring up the mass of our people in the knowledge of the ordinary branches of instruction to which I have adverted, but leave them altogether unprovided with religious training; and not only propose this unheard of scheme, but with great persistency advocate it, and endeavour to force it upon the country.

And the other fact, still more strange and unaccountable, is this, that in a Christian country, the very large majority of the inhabitants of which profess to be believers in Christianity, this most audacious proposal to deprive our population of the benefit of religious education should be for a moment listened to, and not scouted with an almost unanimous rejection. Even now, by the perseverance and artful manœuvres of the opponents of religion, much difficulty and discouragement is caused in a Church school. The notion is spread abroad that religious instruction, instead of being the chief, is of inferior importance to secular knowledge. It has been actually proposed that poor people, who cannot afford to pay for the education of their children, should be *compelled to send them to schools where their own religion is prohibited.* If it were not a fact which is stated in all our newspapers and reported in our parliamentary proceedings, one would think that such a proposal was a foolish joke or mistake. But there is no doubt the thing was really proposed, and at one time it was actually doubtful whether in a House consisting of between 500 and 600 members, nine-tenths of whom would have considered themselves worse than brutes if they did not bring up their own children as Christians, the proposal to educate the children of the poor without religion might not have been adopted by the majority. The atrocious scheme for banishing religion from our schools is but a counterpart of the attempt to prevent men from praying. All I can say is, if such schemes are allowed to succeed, heaven help the next generation! It requires no great power of prophecy to foretell that if religion is banished from our schools, and prayer from our churches, all our civilization, our science and philosophy, all law and order, our domestic peace and happiness, will be extinguished in a flood of anarchy and confusion.

P.S.—The friends of religion appear to me to have made a great mistake in allowing their opponents to form the nomenclature of education. I would venture to propose that for the future all Churchmen should discard the terms "denominational and secular," and use the much more appropriate terms, "Christian" and "non-Christian" education.

CHAPTER XXIV.

THERE are three sorts of language, if not many
more,—Poetical, Popular, and Philosophical,—
each style suited to its special matter. Suppose
we wanted to describe the morning, Virgil would
describe it as

> "Tithoni croceum linquens Aurora cubile,"

that is, "Aurora leaves Tithonus' saffron bed."
Aurora was the wife of Tithonus, and was very
exact at getting up at the first dawn of day.
Dryden says,

> "Now when the rosy Morn began to rise
> And weave her saffron streamer through the skies."

Don Quixote would express himself, "The ruddy
Phœbus begins to spread the golden tresses of
his curly hair over the vast surface of the earthly
globe." Another poet would describe the opening of day as Phœbus yoking the foaming steeds

to his car. A philosopher on the other hand
would say that the break of day was when the
earth had revolved so far on its axis that the disk
of the sun appeared above the horizon.

It is obvious that both these ways of expression would be very unsuitable to ordinary conversation. If you wished your friend to meet
you at early morn, you would not say, "Meet me,
my friend, when Aurora has left Tithonus' rosy
bed," or "when Phœbus has yoked his horses,"
or "mind you get up in good time when the
earth has so far revolved on its axis that the sun's
disk appears above the horizon." You would say,
"Meet me at sunrise," though you would be
using an incorrect expression, because the sun
never does rise.

Now the language of the Bible is often poetical,
more frequently popular, but rarely philosophical.
The eastern languages generally are highly
poetical and figurative. The Psalms of David,
and the books of some of the Prophets contain
perhaps the most highly poetical language that
was ever penned. See the nineteenth Psalm,
beginning, "The heavens declare the glory of
GOD. . . . In them hath He set a tabernacle for
the sun, which cometh forth as a bridegroom out
of his chamber, and rejoiceth as a giant to run his
course." This is, I think, a nobler passage than
Virgil's about "Aurora's saffron couch," or Dry-

den's. So in the Prophet Malachi, "Unto you that fear My Name, the Sun of righteousness shall arise with healing in His wings."

I need not give any examples of the popular style, because almost the whole of the Bible, the historical part especially, is written in that style. It is a simple statement of facts, though here and there interspersed with orientalisms.

But I will select for our consideration a passage not really philosophical, but couched in philosophical language, and illustrative of the non-recognition of strictly philosophical terms when very little of philosophy was known to the people. It is from the Book of the Prophet Jeremiah. "Fear ye not Me? saith the LORD: will ye not tremble at My presence, which have placed the sand for the bound of the sea, by a perpetual decree, that it cannot pass it: and though the waves thereof toss themselves, yet can they not prevail: though they roar, yet can they not pass over it? But this people hath a revolting and rebellious heart." Here the lawlessness of the people is compared with the regular way in which the tides of the mighty ocean conform themselves to the laws which GOD has given them. It is a beautiful poetical illustration, but does not admit of exact application. In fact, the laws of Nature and the moral law of GOD are not strictly similar. Though both may be termed laws in

some sense, as being enacted by the Almighty,
yet subjectively and in respect to the creatures
who have to submit to them, there is an essential
difference. In the one case there is a stringent
necessity, in the other there is a free will which
may or may not submit, and in the present case
does not submit. The tides of the sea follow a
certain law, if for want of a better expression we
choose to call it so. They do God's bidding in a
settled order, except when He chooses to change
it. They cannot help going on at His command.
They cannot help sinking to rest if He should
choose to arrest their violence, as when our Lord
on the sea of Tiberias said unto them, "Peace,
be still." But man is gifted with free agency:
he ought indeed to obey God's command as exactly as the earth in its orbit, or the tides in
their course, but he has the power also, which
they have not, to disobey. Yet the power which
God exercises over the elements might teach him
to fear One so mighty, and not revolt or rebel
against One Who has the power to coerce or to
destroy him. This is the bearing of the passage.

Perhaps there is no more striking instance of
the regularity in which the laws of Nature are
maintained by the great Creator than the tides.
It was necessary to prevent an unhealthy stagnation of the great waters of the sea; and for this
purpose it has been so arranged by the wise and

beneficent Creator that the combined influence of the sun and moon should draw the waters, as it were, " on an heap," sometimes more, sometimes less, so as to cause that wonderful phenomenon of the ebbing and flowing of the tide, and of the spring and neap tide, which presents at once a continual change, and yet a constant regularity.   There is continual change in the tide in accordance with continual changes in the relative position of the sun and moon, and yet the change is within certain limits which cannot be passed.   In the magnificent language of Job, GOD said to the sea, " Hitherto shalt thou come and no further, and here shall thy proud waves be stayed."   It is a striking illustration of the power of GOD which is open to the most uninstructed as well as to the most educated.

But now comes in the philosopher with his matter-of-fact, and objects that the description of the uniformity of the tide, and the unvariableness of the sea-line is not correct.   There are places in the south of England, he will tell us, where the sea has receded two or three miles within the records of history.   The Cinque Ports, which were once the principal harbours on that coast, some of them cannot be approached now.   In other places the sea has gradually encroached upon the land.   And not only so, but there are geological evidences on the coast of Scotland, (not to speak

of other parts of the world,) that there has been
an alternate subsidence and elevation of the land;
so much so, that there are ranges of cliffs evidently once the line of the sea, which are now
fifty or a hundred feet above high water level.

Now this is all perfectly true, and affords a
good instance of the difference between popular
and philosophical language. What is perfectly,
nay strikingly true in a popular or poetical sense,
may possibly not be exactly true in a philosophical
sense. No one gifted with a spark of poetic feeling, nay, no one endowed with common understanding but must recognise the appositeness of
the illustration of the might and unchangeableness
of God contained in the words of the Prophet, in
which He is represented as setting bounds to the
sea, and controlling its fierce waves by His
power. And yet there is no doubt that the
sceptic, if he chooses to raise a cavil, may assert
with truth that there is an inaccuracy of philosophical statement. And this is but an instance of
many other passages, which nevertheless are not
in the smallest degree incompatible with the
truths of God's revealed Word. This is the way
to explain a great number of passages in the
Bible which are perfectly true in their real meaning, but not philosophically accurate.

There is another point connected with the
language of Holy Scripture, which struck me as

very worthy of notice, when I recently saw it mentioned. Supposing that some great philosopher took upon himself to write a children's book, or explain some matter to an uneducated person, —he would use such plain and simple language as was suited to the capacity of the person for whose benefit he wrote or spoke,—and yet it would probably happen that under the garb of this simplicity, matters might crop out, so to speak, inadvertently, which would show that he was much more deeply acquainted with the subject than might at first have been supposed. Such appears to be the case in some parts of Scripture. Take the first chapter of Genesis. It is on the face of it a popular account of the work of creation adapted to the information of simple folk. And yet there appears incidentally allusion to matters which may convey information to the most advanced philosopher or divine. Not to speak however now of the allusion, which all divines recognise, to the doctrine of the plurality of Persons in the Blessed Trinity, there are also traces of a deeper knowledge of philosophy than some are apt to attribute to its inspired author. Until quite recently philosophers knew nothing from science of the order in which the animal world was created, while all the while the exact truth on the subject was contained in the Mosaic narrative. Even now they dispute about the origin of life. Might they not place themselves at the feet of Moses, and learn from him that the impetus which first gave light and life to this inert chaotic mass of mingled land and sea from whence the earth emerged, was the Spirit of GOD. "The Spirit of GOD moved upon the face of the waters, and GOD said, Let there be light, and there was light." The Spirit of GOD was the true moving power which first produced light,—light gave the impulse by GOD's decree and providence to organic life.

Philosophers try very hard to account for the origin of things by the help of some self-evolving power, a notion which to me seems most unphilosophical, if only on the old established principle, "ex nihilo nil fit." I am inclined to think that the time will come when they will admit that Moses was beforehand with them in the true scientific account of Creation.

CHAPTER XXV.

"WHAT a good sermon we had to-day, mamma,"
said a little boy, as he walked home with his mother from church. "My dear," said the lady,
"*all* sermons are good." She meant of course
that preaching is a good and holy institution, and
that it is impertinent for little boys to criticise it.
I fear the criticism of the world is not quite so
respectful. People of the world often complain,
and you may read the same complaints often
in newspapers and periodicals, of the dulness of
sermons. And you may see not unfrequently in
congregations unmistakable evidence of persons
being tired and unable to give their attention,
staring about them, yawning or even sleeping;
some people begin to gape even before the text is
given out.

Now without doubt this feeling of weariness
may arise from the deficiency of the preacher;

s

but it is also, still oftener perhaps, the fault of the hearer. The Apostle explains to us the reason why many persons take no interest in the preaching of the Gospel. "The natural man," he says, "receiveth not the things of the Spirit of GOD, for they are foolishness to him; neither can he know them, because they are spiritually discerned." There must be some sort of sympathy between the speaker and the hearer; or at least between the hearer and that which is addressed to him, or it is not possible for him to take in profitably what he hears. Present the most beautiful picture to a blind man and it is all one as if you placed before him a sheet of blank paper. The man without an ear for music cannot tell the most splendid anthems, operas, or oratorios, one from another. Just so it is with those whose spiritual eyes are blinded, and whose hearts are not attuned to the pure doctrine of the Gospel. It is simply uninteresting to them. They cannot understand it. Take for instance those gentlemen who report or write for newspapers, if they are not religious men. A person has been all the week listening to exciting speeches at public meetings, where the speakers vie with each other in endeavouring to amuse their audience, or he has been where the conflict of political opinion has been raging, and personal altercation has given zest to the debate, when first one speaker and

then another has striven by every art of rhetoric,
whether fair or unfair, to influence the votes of
his hearers, and present to the public the most
favourable view of his case, and this amidst the
cheers of his own party and contrary expressions
of his opponents—or he has been listening in a
Court of Justice to some curious and interesting
trial, in which excitement is wrought up to the
highest pitch, and the life of the criminal, or the
decision of some great cause depends on each
word elicited from the witnesses, or the eloquence
of the counsel, or the summing-up of the judge;
or he has been at a scientific lecture where some
new and wonderful discovery has been described
with the clearest philosophical precision.

After a week of excitement he goes, it may be,
to some quiet parish church where one out of
twenty thousand parish priests speaks to his congregation, as he has spoken for the last twenty
years, not on some matter of worldly excitement,
but on the simple subject of CHRIST Crucified,
and things connected with it.   CHRIST Crucified!
in itself how grand a subject! in itself how worthy of deepest attention—no less than the way
of eternal salvation, the means by which we may
be happy for ever! But alas the demeanour of
a congregation in listening to the preaching of
the Gospel, even when it is earnestly and faithfully preached, is very different from that which

its intrinsic importance might seem to warrant.
Though the subject of our address is the most
momentous affair which can be brought before
human beings, yet it is difficult to give it the
character of reality and interest which is so necessary to rouse attention. Our message, though from
heaven, is an oft told tale. The same persons
have heard the same truths set forth week after
week. The utmost that the preacher can accomplish is by some variety of argument or illustration to prepare the same heavenly food in a more
palatable shape; and even then he will be listened
to rather as one playing on a pleasant instrument,
than as if he were speaking on a subject of vital
importance. On other occasions of public speaking men come together with eager looks, and
anxious minds to hear something in which they
feel that they have a personal interest. But,
strange to say, nothing is more difficult than to
give the real business-like character to a sermon.
One reason of this apathy is that the preacher
speaks of things rather than persons. There is
no personal collision—no excitement of opposition.
And many of the most effectual instruments of
oratory are forbidden. He must not rouse the
passion of his hearers, nor flatter their vanity,
nor give in to their prejudices. There is no place
for sarcasm and invective, or personal attacks, or
amusing anecdotes, or laughter-moving incidents.

All these spirit-stirring topics which are most agreeable to the natural man are excluded from the pulpit.

There is another consideration which operates to the disadvantage of the preacher. An ordinary church congregation is of all audiences the most promiscuous. High and low, rich and poor, educated and illiterate, all have to be instructed, convinced, persuaded. The preacher has to adapt his argument and language to the comprehension and edification of every class, not only in respect to external circumstances, but also as regards spiritual attainment. "It is no easy matter," as an old writer says, "to excite and awaken drowsy souls without terrifying and alarming some tender conscience—to bear home the conviction of sin without the appearance of personal reflection."

One more difficulty there is to which I should allude, namely, that the preacher's business is to create not only a powerful but a permanent effect —not barely cause a transient qualm of conscience, a momentary ebullition of feeling, but to make a lasting impression on the heart, and effect a corresponding change of conduct. This point is essential, and if we look at this point only, how far easier is the task of every other speaker than that of the preacher. The advocate has gained his point when he has obtained a verdict for his

client. It matters not what may be the opinion
of the jury to-morrow. The speaker at the elec-
tion, or convivial party, or public meeting has
generally little more to do than to ingratiate himself with his partizans by expressing sentiments
congenial with their own. When the last cheer
has died away his task is done. But with the
Christian preacher a permanent effect is everything. What he says to his congregation ought
to have an influence for eternity.

Hence it is that the words of the preacher are
so unimpressive to the "natural man"—the mere
man of the world : they do not harmonize with
his tone of thought, his feelings, his prejudices—
they are foolishness to him. They do not furnish
him with the excitement which he needs. His
mind is set on earthly things—the pursuits of the
world are to him all in all. The method of salvation, the doctrines and precepts of the Gospel
have for him little charm. These are the sort of
men who sneer at the preaching of the Gospel,
ignorant all the while that the fault lies in their
own inaptitude for spiritual things.

And yet there is another view of the preaching
of the Gospel. "It pleased GOD by the foolishness of preaching to save them that believe."
The despisers of preaching seem to forget that
the preaching of the Gospel of CHRIST has in
reality effected the greatest moral revolution which

the world ever witnessed. The first preachers of
the Gospel literally "turned the world upside
down." They reformed the barbarous customs of
the Pagan world, closed the temples of the Heathen Gods, shut up the schools of philosophers.
The doctrine which they taught is the basis of the
civilization of modern society; and though, to the
ear of the sceptic, there may be little interest in
the words of the preacher, and though there may
be restless countenances and drowsy looks amongst
many a congregation, yet it is most certain that
the words of the preacher have often sunk deep
into the heart of many a conscience-stricken
sinner; many a poor sinful man has gone home
and fallen on his knees before GOD, and the sermon, much despised by the philosopher sceptic,
has been the blessed means of converting that
man from a life of sin to one of righteousness.

To take even a more ordinary common-place
sort of view. It has been shrewdly remarked by a
celebrated lawyer that the preachers of the Gospel
have a great advantage in the privilege of addressing fifty thousand sermons to the people every
year, *without the opportunity of a reply*. That is
most true. To this circumstance we may attribute much of the permanency of the Christian
faith and of whatever good conduct exists amongst
us. What would be the state of this country, or
of any country in the world, if the people had no

religious instruction, and were not reminded continually of death and judgment, and of their duties to GOD and man? We may form some notion if we look at the fearful state of some of our great towns, or of the condition of society where Christianity has been put down by popular violence. Imagine the condition of England under such a state of things. There would spring up a state of diabolical savagery such as the world has not hitherto witnessed. Oh, it is a blessing beyond price to be reminded once a week of GOD and of eternity, even if the preacher has not the gift of eloquence.

CHAPTER XXVI.

FUTURE RETRIBUTION.—MOST CHARITABLE TO DECLARE IT PLAINLY AS IT IS DECLARED IN THE BIBLE.

NOTHING more irritates the philosophic sceptic than the doctrine of eternal punishment, especially punishment for unbelief. Nothing provokes louder protestations of aversion. We may be permitted to surmise that these protestations arise not unfrequently from a suspicion that there is only too much truth in what so much annoys them. Men seek by the loudness of their exclamation to pretend at least that they have no fear —as the countryman will shout and whistle as he passes by the village churchyard, or as the child will keep up his courage by singing in the dark.

But the philosopher should at least refrain from feelings of irritation against GOD's ministers who remind him of these truths. He should consider that if the terrors of the judgment are, as Christian divines verily believe, most true, it would be an act of the greatest injustice and cowardice if, for fear of disapproval, they in any way concealed them. The Gospel of the LORD JESUS CHRIST is indeed a dispensation of mercy—tidings of great joy, a message of forgiveness and reconciliation, the love of GOD to man; yea, it is all this—every page of the Gospel abounds in love. And yet in no part of Holy Scripture is there such severe denunciation of GOD's wrath against sin, nowhere such stern threatenings of judgment against the impenitent. Not even the most vehement of the ancient prophets used stronger language of severity against the wicked, than that which proceeds out of the mouth of the merciful JESUS. "Woe unto you, Pharisees, hypocrites," He says, "ye fools and blind . . . . Ye serpents, ye generation of vipers, how shall ye escape the damnation of hell?" So in the description of the last judgment, "Depart from Me, ye cursed, into everlasting fire, prepared for the devil and his angels." The Apostles use the same language. S. Paul speaks with special severity against those who pervert the Gospel of CHRIST, "There be some," he says, "that trouble you and pervert the Gospel of CHRIST. But though an angel from heaven preached any other Gospel to you than that which we have preached to you, let him be accursed." At the end of his First Epistle to the Corinthians he actually takes the pen from his amanuensis and writes with his own hand,—

" If any man love not the LORD JESUS, let him be Anathema, Maran-atha.   The grace of our LORD JESUS CHRIST be with you.   My love be with you all in CHRIST JESUS, Amen."   The greater his love for the brethren, the stronger is his language of denunciation against those who seduce them from the love of GOD.

Now what I would ask of those who talk of want of charity and bigotry, and so forth, is whether a minister of the Gospel or any serious Christian, who really believes that this is the language of inspiration, and that the souls of men are to be judged according to GOD's Word, and yet suppresses or softens down GOD's declarations of eternal wrath against sin, can escape the charge of hypocrisy or cowardice.

It is easy enough to understand how the present morbid feeling on the subject has sprung up. In an age of unexampled wealth and prosperity, men have become so immersed in the pursuits of this life, so wholly taken up with its pleasures, and comforts, and excitements, that they cannot bear to be reminded of the time when their enjoyments will have an end, and they will have to give a strict account of the deeds done in the flesh.   The curses of GOD on the impenitent, the eternal pains of hell, seem to them words unsuited to ears polite.   They do not like to have the subject pressed upon them, and seek for arguments

to explain it away. It is not to be wondered at
that men who have given their souls to mere
worldly philosophy, and put from them the belief
in GOD's revealed Word, should find arguments
to convince those who desire to be convinced.
But it is marvellous that men who have accepted
GOD's commission to preach the Gospel should
dare to deny or explain away the very doctrines
which they have pledged themselves to teach.
The Church, more faithful than some of her ministers, shrinks not from plainly setting forth
GOD's curses as well as His blessings. "Cursed
is he that removeth his neighbour's landmark,"
whether literally, or by unsettling his belief in
spiritual truth. "Cursed is he that maketh the
blind to go out of his way"—a fearful warning
to the clever man of the world, who recklessly
suggests doubts and difficulties to the unlearned.
"Cursed are the unmerciful, fornicators, adulterers, covetous persons, idolaters, slanderers,
drunkards, and extortioners." Good men do not
sufficiently show their indignation against those
who go about corrupting the faith of the unsus-
pecting. Intellect and wealth are the great idols
of the day. If a man has secured to himself an
abundance of this world's wealth, and contributes
to the amusement and vanity of his neighbour,
too little is thought of his religious character.
So even more strikingly in the so-called world of

intellect, there is far too little account made of this most vital point. The ingenious sceptic, the man who takes a perverse delight in placing revelation and science in apparent discrepancy—the man who scruples not to promulgate anti-Christian theories, which, though confessedly unsupported by ascertained facts, he blurts forth with hardy unconcern whether they be tenable, or, after all, exploded as nonsense, and in the meantime, with a selfish carelessness of the ruin which he may cause to immortal souls by his rash speculation, enjoys the applause of men as reckless and frivolous as himself,—these, and such as these, if they are only clever, are welcomed with the same favour, as those who by their well-regulated talents are doing God service, and advancing the true interest of the human race.

In declaring God's eternal wrath against sin and unbelief, we must not allow the caviller the advantage of saying that the Apostle, and those who accept his words as truth, condemn to God's eternal reprobation all those in every country and in every age of the world who do not think exactly as they do themselves. We are bound to accept with faith and humble gratitude the terms of God's unbounded mercy in CHRIST. But there have been, and still are, millions of the earth's inhabitants who have never heard of CHRIST. How can such as these believe without hearing,

and how can they love Him of whom they have
not heard? Evidently the denunciations of Scripture cannot apply to them—they have a law unto
themselves. If they have no part in the salvation
of the faithful, so neither have they any part in
the condemnation of unbelievers. There may be,
even in a Christian land, many who come under
the same category as heathens. We cannot say.
But in all appearance there are many so adversely
circumstanced that, though no doubt they have
heard the Name of CHRIST uttered, perhaps in
blasphemy, yet morally the alternative has never
been presented to them of accepting or not accepting CHRIST as their SAVIOUR. No; the
Apostle is evidently speaking of those who have
known CHRIST intellectually, yet put Him from
them, or love Him not—men who have been
called, yet reject the calling—men to whom the
preaching of the Gospel is foolishness—disputers
of this world—wise men, who, with all their
wisdom, know not GOD—the "natural man, who
receiveth not the things of the Spirit of GOD"—
men of carnal minds—wise men, taken in their
own craftiness—men who have just cleverness
enough to persuade themselves to be infidels—
men who, having had CHRIST and the Resurrection preached to them, cavil at GOD's revelation,
and ask, "How are the dead raised up, and with
what body do they come?"—philosophic infidels

—men of Sadducean mind. It is a fearful and
humiliating thought that all such as these are
classed in the same condemnation as "the un-
righteous, fornicators, idolaters, adulterers, effeminate, thieves, covetous, drunkards," and such
like. It is a lamentable truth that pride of intellect, not less than grosser sins, should thus
involve men in hopeless condemnation; yet there
can be no question of it, according to the plain
Word of GOD.

What an alternative for the proud, highly-
informed, enlightened man of the present day—
the despiser of the Church's holy faith, the liberal
tolerater of all denominations, who looks upon
Christian doctrine as something which men may
receive or reject as they please, and either turns
from it altogether, or frames a creed for himself accepting such doctrines as appear to him
reasonable, and despising others—what a humiliating alternative for such an one to be told that
rejecting the Catholic faith, refusing to believe
the Gospel he must without doubt perish everlastingly; or, if he escape eternal wrath it can
only be through the loopholes of invincible ignorance or involuntary prejudice! Yet such, if
GOD's Word is true, such, if the Church founded
by the Apostles have not altogether erred—such
unquestionably is the only alternative whereby
those persons can in any way be saved who

reject or disbelieve the truth as it is revealed
by God.

Even so the philosophers of ancient Greece,
intellectual, highly accomplished, full of knowledge and learning—these men looked on the
Cross of Christ as foolishness, contemned the
doctrine of Christ's messengers, and perished in
their sin. How many able, accomplished, philosophical men are there in the present day who
are in like danger! How many who are loudest
in their complaint about the ignorance and vices
of the poor, are yet entirely blind to their own!
How many even who pay great attention to
schemes of philanthropy, promoters of education,
and other plans of utility, yet, because they reject
God's eternal Truth, the doctrines of that Gospel
which Christ revealed, and which the Church
has taught must, without hope, without remedy,
perish ; unless—unless, O strange and hazardous
alternative! Christ should plead before the Father for their forgiveness, on account of the
gross impenetrable darkness in which their souls
were involved!

This is one of the most difficult tasks of the
Christian minister—to preach a doctrine so un-
popular, so paradoxical, yet so unquestionably
true. And not only to preach it in the pulpit,
but to show elsewhere that he looks with a sad,
uncordial aspect on those, however high in sta-

tion, exalted in intellect, admirable even in their philanthropy, who are aliens to the Christian faith, viewing them as men who, in spite of their talents and advantages, are not doing the LORD's work in their generation, but rather thwarting it, and if they repent not and accept the terms of the Gospel, must, through GOD's just sentence, perish everlastingly.

T

CHAPTER XXVII.

UNRESTRAINED INQUIRY LEADS TO THE MOST OPPOSITE RESULTS.—THE INTELLECTUAL POWERS OF MAN NEED RELIGION FOR THEIR DEVELOPMENT.—THE LABOURER, THE MERCHANT, THE STATESMAN, THE PHILOSOPHER.

I REMEMBER at the beginning of the "Church movement" some forty years ago, when great zeal sprang up for "Church principles," and many subjects of thought, which had been well-nigh forgotten were revived, the more cautious men endeavoured somewhat to restrain the impetuosity of their friends, suggesting that they were wandering into dangerous fields of inquiry. I remember myself writing a very urgent letter on the subject to Archbishop Manning—before his secession—but to no effect. The usual answer was that it was the duty of all men to follow after truth whithersoever it might take them, and not shrink from any inquiry, or any phase of thought or action which might lead to it. The result was, that after a few years some of the leading men of the movement became Ultramontanes.

A similar process is going on in the domain of science. Philosophers assert that the first duty of man is inquiry after truth at all events. "Not to inquire," says a very moderate writer, "was possible for our forefathers, but is not possible for us. With our intellectual growth has come an irrepressible anxiety to possess the highest truth attainable by us. The desire is not sinful, not presumptuous, but really one of the best and purest of our instincts, being nothing else than the sterling honesty of the intellect seeking the harmony of discordant truth."[1] Yet we know that this sort of thing has led not a few in recent times to Atheism or infidelity.

Here is a curious phase of the human mind. The same principle of unrestrained, it may be conscientious inquiry after truth, has made some men infidels and some Ultramontanes. And these men of the highest intellect in their respective departments. The leading men among the Roman Catholics in this country, and some of the foremost philosophers of the day, have been brought by the very same principle of following, as they supposed, the path of truth, to diverge to the most opposite points of intellectual position. How do we account for this? It is quite clear that inquiry after truth, good as it must be

[1] See "The Intellectual Life," by Philip Gilbert Hamerton, p. 211.

confessed to be in itself, yet may be productive of evil. How is this?

First, it is the law of Nature, or rather the ordainment of God's Providence that what is good will, if unrestrained, run out to vicious excess. " 'Tis good to have a giant's strength, but not to use it as a giant." Money is a good thing—all of us have to seek for the means of subsistence; but if we rush into the pursuit of wealth with such unrestrained eagerness as to make gold our idol, we fall away to moral degradation. Strong drink is good, "wine maketh glad the heart of man," but we know that thousands of our labouring men are ruining body and soul by drunkenness.

The truth is that in all things, even in the pursuit of knowledge, there is need of ballast; there is need of moral restraint to control the intellectual impulse. What says the wise man in praise of wisdom, "Wisdom is the principal thing, therefore get wisdom. . . . Happy is the man that findeth wisdom, and the man that getteth understanding." And he adds elsewhere, "The fear of the LORD is the beginning of wisdom."

Let the philosopher of the present day well consider this. It is the secret of intellectual as well as moral culture. It is most true, as I have myself heard excellent men of science affirm, that we ought to follow after truth wheresoever it leads us,—but then we must have the fear of GOD for our ballast, or we shall fall into the extremes of infidelity or fanaticism. The intellect of man without this fear of GOD as a principle of action, is so weak, and temptation to evil is so universally present, even in purely intellectual pursuits, that we shall surely fall into grievous error, if our hearts are not guided by the fear of the LORD, that is, the true religious principle.

Now is the boasted knowledge of the present day built on the fear of GOD? Is there not on the contrary in too many a careless neglect, or presumptuous rejection of all that appertains to the fear of GOD; a vain reliance on their own powers,—a leaning to their own understanding,—a sort of half unwilling acknowledgment that religion may be all very well in its own proper department, but that it is misplaced when it interferes with intellectual pursuits?

By the fear of GOD we are not to understand a slavish and superstitious dread of GOD. It is a very different thing from superstition; it is most worthy of a rational, free, and intelligent being. It is a reverence and veneration for Him on account of His wisdom, power, and goodness; an acknowledgment of His superintending Providence. To live in the fear of GOD is to go through life, not with a continual apprehension of GOD's

wrath, but with a perpetual assurance of His
goodness. In short, the fear of the LORD is the
religious feeling of a good man. It is the ground-
work of the right reason of an intelligent being.
In Christian language it is much the same as
faith,—faith as distinguished from superstition
on the one hand, and scepticism on the other.

It is religion that gives us a just estimate of
our real condition in the world. It alone can
conquer the inherent pride of the human heart,
and enable us to think humbly of ourselves as
we ought to think. It has been most truly said,
that "the greatest wisdom may often be to know
our own ignorance."

Religion alone can subdue those angry passions and violent lusts which destroy our natural
sense of right and wrong. What is the cause of
all the wrong-headedness, obstinacy, folly and
madness of the world around us? Spring they
not from the domination of evil passions which
pervert and obscure the judgment? How utterly
incompetent is a man under the influence of a
master passion to judge rightly or consult wisely.
What absurd arguments do men bring forward,
—how unable are they to discern what is right
and wrong when swayed by the violent counsels
of party spirit or prejudice. It is religion alone
which can calm the turbulent waves which rage
and swell in our hearts, and say to the tempest

of excited passions, Peace, be still. It is religion
alone which can dispel the selfishness inherent in
the human heart, and teach us that true wisdom
consists in foregoing our own selfish advantages,
and loving our neighbours as ourselves.

All these qualities which are essential to the
free and unbiassed use of our reason, and the
exercise of useful practical wisdom—religion, or
the fear of GOD alone can give.

And how does the fear of GOD enlarge the
sphere of man's intellectual vision. It places before him a multitude of high and holy topics, of
which he who fears not GOD is entirely ignorant
and incompetent to judge. Look at the hus-
bandman whose daily occupation is to till the
earth,—how low in the scale of intellectual beings
is that man, if he knows not GOD, and cares
only to satisfy the cravings of his natural appetites! how little superior is he to the swine
which feed under the oak tree without ever looking up to know from whence their food was sent.
But let that man be instructed in the fear of
GOD, let the truths of the Bible be unfolded to
him, let him give his soul to the influence of
religion,—what a change is wrought in his whole
inner man! How is his whole soul enlarged!
How does his very occupation, otherwise so dry
and barren, so toilsome and tedious, serve to im-
press upon him the wonders of GOD's Providence,

when He sends the former and the latter rain, and maketh the sun to shine, and the seed to germinate, and the ear to fill. What a different intellect is his from that of the mere sensual animal who eats, and drinks, and sleeps, and works, and knows not God.

Look at the tradesman or merchant; see him first poring over his ledger and day-book, his mind wholly given to buying and selling, computing his losses and profits. What a life of sordid drudgery is this without religion. But suppose that man, by Divine grace, to be influenced by the fear of God, behold an expansive field of intellectual acquirement opened to him. What a noble range of speculation for the mind, what sublime, what soul-inspiring topics to dwell on in comparison with the dry details in which his soul was before wrapped up. What a relief after the tedious business of worldly gain to hold communion with God, and ponder on His word and works. This indeed is true wisdom, "The merchandise of it is better than the merchandise of silver, and the gain thereof than fine gold."

Look again at the statesman: consider first the narrow-minded party politician, how utterly unable is he to distinguish between the real good of his country, and the petty interests of his political faction. He regards not his fellow-countrymen as beings endowed with immortal imperishable souls. He regards them in the masses, as instruments for increasing the nation's wealth, or supporters or opposers of this or that system of policy. He thinks not of them as " brethren for whom CHRIST died," heirs of immortality, aspirants to equality with the angels. Alas for the nation whose interests are placed in the hands of men who know not GOD !

But picture to yourselves the statesman whose soul is enlarged by the fear of GOD. What a different intellect do we behold. How far nobler a view does he take of a nation's good. His object is to make the nation over which GOD has placed him more moral, more religious, more fit for GOD's eternal kingdom. He will not pander to the people's passions, but makes the law of GOD his rule of conduct. He takes his straightforward unbending course of highest duty, firmly trusting that GOD will prosper that which is undertaken and finished in His Name.

Once more, look at the philosopher who knows not GOD,—cannot even "think" of Him,—regards the material world as under no providential rule, but carried on by some fate or blind necessity—who knows not whence he came, or whither he goes after this life,—imagines that man—intellectual man—was developed from an ape, and after this life is resolved into his original elements, and lives no more,—why what a mean

and miserable view of things is this. Contrast
with it the glorious revelations of the blessed
Word of GOD—which tells us of man, formed in
the image of GOD, redeemed from sin and death,
—a place prepared for him in the kingdom of
heaven.

Thus in every department of life religion, or
the fear of GOD, is the grand enlightener of the
human intellect, the source of all true wisdom.
In short, a man without religion is but half a
man, intellectually—morally he is a good deal
worse than nothing.

CHAPTER XXVIII.

PROGRESS.—ARTS AND SCIENCE MAY ADVANCE INDEFI-
NITELY, BUT CHRIST'S TRUE RELIGION REMAINS THE
SAME ALWAYS.

A CURIOUS fallacy has sprung up in the minds of
modern philosophers, namely, that because the
world has lately made great advancement in art
and science, therefore it must needs have made
great advancement in other things. It is easy to
perceive at once that this is a logical *non sequitur*;
yet it may be well to give our thoughts to a consideration of the matter.

There can be no question that the age we live
in has made a wonderful start forward in the
knowledge of material objects. In truth, unless
a generation of men were very stupid indeed they
must always be advancing onwards in this department, because each generation has the advantage
of the attainments of those who have gone before
it, and is continually building on the foundation
which they have laid. As Professor Small well
said at the recent meeting of the British Association, "It was not too much to say that without

the treatise of the Greek geometer on conic sections there would have been no Kepler—without Kepler no Newton, and without Newton no science in our modern signification, at least no such conception of nature as now lay at the basis of all our science of nature, as subject in its smallest as well as its greatest phenomena to exact quantitative relation, and to definite numerical laws." Unless indeed there should be some breaking up of the framework of society, some period of convulsion, or of darkness, the human mind will be always adding to its store of knowledge. There was a period after the destruction of the Roman Empire by the Gothic nations, when the advancement almost ceased, nay, the world went back rather than forward. Arts which had been known to the ancient world were forgotten, most of its literature perished, and, unless the Church had kept alive the lamp of learning and science, knowledge would have died out and become almost extinguished. So it would be if the present system of society were broken up by revolution and anarchy; there would be a temporary cessation of the progress of art and science and all things. The advance of atheism would be a reaction towards ignorance.

The great advance of the present age is in science and those arts which depend on science. When once the art of printing was discovered and generally used, the publication of books was multiplied and increased rapidly, until we have arrived at the present astonishing development of literature. So when the power of steam was ascertained, its wondrous capabilities were soon applied to the variety of objects for which it is now used in manufactures, commerce, and locomotion. There seems no end of the uses to which it may be applied. The discovery and great improvement of the telescope and microscope enabled men to make new and marvellous discoveries both in the grandeur and minuteness of the material world.

Resulting from the advancement of science has been the development of those arts which minister to the temporal well-being of the present generation. The constantly increasing number of families who enjoy the blessings of competency, the rapid erection of comfortable dwellings, and, even in the poorest families where moderate thrift and prudence are exercised, the enjoyment of many comforts which were unknown to former generations.

But because we have attained acknowledged superiority in these matters, does it therefore follow that we are wiser or better than our fathers in other respects? Because science has taught us to rule the elements, are we better able to rule our own passions and curb the madness of the

people? Because improved art and machinery
supply our dwellings with comforts and conveniences unknown to former ages, are our minds
therefore better stored with moral wisdom, or our
conduct to GOD and our neighbour better ordered?
The mechanic who governs by his skill the great
power of the steam engine, is he on that account
more skilled in the guidance of the social machine,
or one whit more practically versed in the power
of GOD over the moral universe? Surely no comparison can be drawn between subjects wide as
the poles asunder. No; let us concede to the
present generation all the praise which it deserves
for enlarging the boundaries of science, and advancing the arts to unknown perfection, but let
us not vainly suppose that we are wiser or better
than our forefathers in matters unconnected with
the department of either art or science.

There are a good many drawbacks to the advantages conferred on the world by the advancement of art and science. Enervating luxury
amongst the rich, improvidence, and consequent
suffering amongst the poor, these sadly mar the
blessings which Providence has showered upon
us. Then again, the skill and energy which have
enabled men of the present day to increase so
largely the comforts of peace, have also developed
in at least an equal degree the arts of war. It is
a sad reflection that as much ingenuity and skill

and energy should be devoted to improve the
implements of destruction, as to increase the
comforts of life—to construct iron-clad batteries,
enormously destructive guns, arms calculated to
destroy the greatest number of our fellow-creatures, in the smallest possible time.   Take again
the immense mass of information spread by the
art of printing amidst our teeming population.
What is the source of the supposed information
which the majority of men possess?   Is it not
notorious that it is derived from the daily and
weekly press, journals, pamphlets, magazines, reviews, "Penny Awfuls," &c.   Can any more
copious fountain of error be conceived?   Is it
not notorious that the press—especially the lower
kind of the periodical press—is a most mendacious
source of information?   Of course there are many
excellent and trustworthy publications.   But what
must we say of the organs of parties?   Is it not
their daily business to inflame the passions, flatter
the vanity, and pander to the appetites of their
own particular readers?   What perversion, what
misstatement, what exaggeration, what wilful
falsehood, what absurd ignorance!   and this is the
fountain from which streams the boasted intelligence of the present generation.   Alas for our
ignorance and delusion!   We may talk of the
superstitious credulity of our uneducated forefathers, we may sneer at their veneration for old-

established usages, and laugh at their belief in
witchcraft. I will venture to say without the
slightest qualification that never was there an
age in which the mass of mankind listened to
falsehood with such implicit credulity—such utter
prostration of intellect—never was there an age
in which so many barefaced lies were published
and believed as the present.

But I am wandering rather from my subject,
which was to show that the great increase of
knowledge in arts and science which exists in the
present day, does not imply a large advance in
matters unconnected with art and science, in fact,
that there are many things which have not advanced at all, but have rather retrograded.   Take
by way of illustration the art of sculpture. Sculpture is the delineation in marble of the highest
beauties of the human form.   In ancient Greece
where great attention was paid to the graceful
development of the limbs, which were much more
exposed to view than they are at present ; the art
of sculpture arrived at once at its highest excellence, so that no modern sculptors have attained
the same proficiency in their art as Phidias and
Praxiteles.   Take again the art of language; no
one pretends that any modern language comes
up to the excellency of the Greek; and language
is no inconsiderable test of acuteness of intellect.
So in poetry. I venture to think that Tenny-

son and Browning cannot compete with Homer and Æschylus.

You see then that advancement in all things is not at all the property of the present age. We have advanced there is no doubt in arts and science, but then there are other things in which we have rather retrograded.

All that I have said tends to the question whether in the highest department of human excellence —that is religion—we can be said to have advanced or retrograded. Is a good Christian now a different sort of man from a good Christian in the time of S. Paul and the Apostles, or is he not precisely the same ? Was it not possible for a Christian to attain to the highest excellence of his calling in the first ages of Christianity ? As the Greek sculptor was able to delineate the perfect form of human symmetry, such as no future ages could surpass, so was not the perfect stature of the Christian attained, so far as it is attainable at all, in the first .ages of the Gospel ? I think there cannot be more than one answer—that the Apostles of our LORD and many of the early converts attained at least as high excellence of moral virtue as any of those who have lived in later ages.

And if so, then I have a further question to ask, namely, what was the cause of this excellence —but their reception in its integrity of the perfect law of GOD, the bringing their hearts into subjection to the Christian doctrine? From whence it follows that Christianity itself was from the beginning perfect and entire, wanting nothing, and that the notion of religious knowledge developing itself, like modern art and science, is perfectly untenable. God revealed Himself in CHRIST in all His perfection. The notion that modern science can unfold to us a more perfect knowledge of God than the Bible does, is untrue. As individuals indeed we should be continually aiming at greater excellence, greater conformity to the holy Will of God, and the perfect example of our SAVIOUR. We should take the energy and zeal of the man of science as examples for ourselves. The same energy and perpetual progress which distinguish the philosopher should be aimed at by each one of us in the concerns of his soul. We should never be content with low attainment, always aspiring after something better, some advancement in our spiritual state. We should be continually subduing within us everything inconsistent with our Christian calling, and advancing onward in the course toward perfection.

You see then that in this point of view the Christian course is eminently one of progress. If we admire the energy of the men of the present generation, applaud their discoveries and recognize the necessity of continual advancement; if we would advance the well-being of the generation in which we live, we should be constantly endeavouring to increase the influence of true religion whether national or personal, constantly pulling down the strong holds of sin, and building up the fabric of CHRIST's holy religion around and within us.

It will perhaps be said that though the Gospel may have been delivered full and entire at first, yet that the labours of learned men are very valuable to elucidate and explain religious truth. Yes, but their object is not to improve what is perfect, but simply to bring it back to its original excellence. When the Bishops of the Church assembled at Nicæa their object was not to construct anything anew, but to bear testimony as to what had been the belief of the Church from the beginning. So at the Reformation: the professed object was to restore the Church to its original excellence. And so in this present day ·the object of learned men is not to add to the Gospel, but to restore manuscripts to their original purity, to discover what was the meaning of those from whom we have received them, to ascertain the mind of the Prophets and Apostles, and of Him by whose inspiration they wrote. Human science may advance onward continually. Human art may go on from one degree of perfection to another—but Eternal Truth never changes. The Gospel is like its Divine Author, "Jesus Christ, the same yesterday, to-day, and for ever."

Note.—I would not be understood to contradict the sentiments so eloquently expressed by Canon Lightfoot in the debate on "Theological Thought" at the recent Congress at Bath. "The great truths of revealed religion remain in themselves the same from age to age. But an apprehension of them and an appreciation of them, an application of them to the emergent needs of the individual and of society, in the more complex and trying circumstances of modern times may and ought to vary, and that in the direction of ever-increasing growth, and grateful realization."

What I maintain is, that Christian doctrine and principle and Christian character are one and the same always; though they must of course be adapted to the ever-varying needs of the human family—and this, not as some seem to expect, by bending or giving way to the supposed discoveries of philosophy—but by the mild and efficacious persuasion of Christian Truth in its various aspects, bringing all, whether learned or unlearned, under the influence of Christian principles and salvation through the blessed Gospel. This is very different from what was said by Prebendary Gale, that "Theology has no finality. It is never the same; it is absolutely endless; it is fresh every morning; it requires a new interpretation every year we live." These sentiments I am happy to say were received by the assembly with "No" and laughter.

CHAPTER XXIX.

As I began, so I conclude, by expressing my
earnest wish that men who seem intended by
nature, or rather by GOD's Providence to work
together for the glory of GOD, could be brought
to unite in the service of Him Who gave them all
the gifts which they possess. It is the bounden
duty and the high office of GOD's priests to win
men to the knowledge of the truth, and induce
them to rule their lives in obedience to His laws.
Scarcely less noble and divine is the work of the
true philosopher, to investigate the wonders of
GOD's creation, and explain its marvels. Why
cannot men, bound together as it would seem
by such a chain of love and high emprise, work
harmoniously in the great path of duty which is
set before them?

I fear there are some—a few, I would fain
hope—who deliberately and of fixed purpose set
themselves to oppose GOD's ministers; and that
under a false notion that they are in some way
throwing impediments in the path of science.

But surely it is an altogether mistaken thought. Even if they would, the clergy have not the power to check the march of science in her grand discoveries, nay, rather, they would willingly hail philosophy as their best ally in winning men to a knowledge of GOD's glorious works. It is one of the most unfortunate circumstances of the day, that some men of science should have taken up these atheistical opinions. I really do not think they are more than some half-score, but then they are leading men; and others equally or more able let them have their way far more than they ought, instead of protesting against them, and making them ashamed. In the case of such persons as these, who wilfully oppose the truth, GOD's ministers have no alternative. They would basely desert their post, if they did not first endeavour to set before the opponents of the truth, the fatal issue to themselves of the course which they are pursuing, in the hope of yet, by GOD's mercy, winning them to His service. And if they fail, then, by all means in their power they must warn those who are in danger of being deceived by them, against the fallacies and false doctrines which are put before them. This I have endeavoured to do with plainness and earnestness of speech,—and I pray GOD that my words may not be altogether in vain.

I have carefully endeavoured to avoid the ex-

ample of those philosophers who allow themselves
to use the most insulting expressions against the
clergy as a class. Whenever I have spoken
strongly, it is simply against the doctrines of
those mistaken men, who, in my conscience, I
believe are destroying the souls of those for whom
CHRIST died.

But there is another class to whom, in a great
measure, my words of remonstrance are addressed.
I mean those excellent and able men, who have
no intention whatever of forsaking their religion
in the pursuit of science—or of leading others to
unbelief in GOD's Word—and yet do, unwittingly
but most seriously, damage the cause of truth, by
seeming to side with its enemies. These are men
of science, eminent in their department, and they
are also Christians. What I grieve for is, that
they should seem to forsake their brethren in the
faith, and side with the enemies of GOD. Surely
their Christianity is of greater moment than their
philosophy; one is but material, the other spiritual; one is temporal, the other for eternity.
I would appeal to men of science who are really
Christians, to range themselves, more decidedly
than they do, on the LORD's side, not to suffer
the interests of their worldly pursuit to bias them
against those who are doing the LORD's work.
It is possible that instances may be quoted in
which priests, more zealous than well-informed,

have thwarted the discoveries of men of science—
as in the often quoted case of Galileo—though I
confess I never heard of a similar instance of per-
secution for science' sake, while it is notorious
that thousands of Christian martyrs have perished
for religion's sake. But there is no disposition
in the present day to check the discoveries of
science, and no power, if any one desired, to do
so. Let men of science put from them this unworthy jealousy.

But it is not only to men of science that I
would address myself, but generally to the men
of intelligence and culture. We all acknowledge,
at least all Christians acknowledge, that there is
a great spiritual battle to be fought in the world
between good and evil. Every human soul is
engaged in the conflict. We are bound to fight
manfully as sworn soldiers of the cross. But
there are some who have deserted their colours,
and what is still worse, do all they can to induce
others to desert. I do say, without hesitation,
that it is the duty of every Christian who has a
grain of faith in his SAVIOUR, to set himself
against such men, and discourage and counteract
their proceedings. What is the value of all these
discoveries in art and science? what is the worth
of the most important of material and worldly interests, if they are leading men away from their
faith in CHRIST, and their allegiance to their

GOD ?   It is notorious and undeniable that there are men of science who are working, as we Christians believe, for the damnation of souls.   I say that such men should be shrunk from with aversion.   If indeed we can by any means induce them to desist from their ungodly endeavours, it is our duty in charity to aid them ; but if they persist in spreading opinions which we in our conscience believe to be ruining souls, and tending to the destruction of all that we love and value even in this world, it does seem to be the very height of moral cowardice and folly to countenance—nay, even flatter men like them, who, if suffered to go on in their present course, bid fair to revolutionize society both morally and physically, and bring the world back to savagery and anarchy.

I pray GOD to avert such threatening calamity, and beseech all earnest men to weigh the words which I have spoken, and aid in the promotion of what they verily believe to be GOD's Truth.

It is not that we clergy claim the right to interfere with men's opinions otherwise than by persuasion.   Politically and individually men may hold what opinions they choose, on their own responsibility.   What we complain of is, that these men are interfering with us, and with those whom GOD has commissioned us to instruct in the way of Truth—that by rash and false specula-

tions they are leading them to ruin, bringing in
notions which will lead to the most deplorable
results in the world, and spreading through the
the social system "a monstrous and melancholy
atheism."

Surely it is our bounden duty to raise our
voice, if possible, in language as strong and uncompromising as that of the ancient prophets of
Israel—or in whatever way we may hope to obtain
a hearing—to use our best endeavours, by the
help of GOD, to oppose and check this unhappy
tendency, and to rescue the souls committed to
our charge from the dangers which have invaded
them ; and to call on all right-minded persons to
aid us by all the means in their power to rescue
society from this direfully impending calamity.

I am quite aware that in the foregoing papers
there are some things which will displease sceptical or unbelieving philosophers, and if they are
ill-tempered, as well as unbelieving, they will
throw the book away in a rage.   But it is impossible to write with equal force and propriety with
different objects in view.   My object is not so
much to win unbelievers, as to warn others against
them.   If my chief object had been to conciliate
unbelievers, I might have omitted some topics on
which I have insisted.   I might have refrained
from quoting against them the uncourteous and
contemptuous language which they use towards

the clergy. I might have thought it better not to jest on some of the notions which have been adopted by certain modern philosophers, but which appear to most people to be supremely ridiculous. But if I had omitted these topics, I should have missed the principal object which I have in view, which is to warn the unwary, but perhaps well-meaning persons of the present day, against the danger which lurks under modern speculations, if they be not conducted in the fear of GOD. One of the worst features of the times is the way in which clever men are flattered without reference to their principles. I have endeavoured conscientiously to avoid this error, and to speak in true and righteous terms both of the great value of philosophy, rightly so called, and the extreme wrong done by those who prostitute it to atheistic uses ; and at the same time to show that the salvation of souls and the honour of GOD, are the highest and noblest objects of human endeavours.

Philosophy falsely so called—the hater and opponent of Christianity, is an evil thing—as the Apostle says, " earthly, sensual, devilish."

True philosophy, springing from "meekness of wisdom," the ally and promoter of GOD's eternal Truth, is excellent and honourable in the sight of GOD and man.

NOTE A. (P. 73.)

DESCENT OF MAN.

Two arguments have lately struck me as strongly contradicting the notion of man's evolution from an ape. Some philosophers are fond of asserting the slight difference which they suppose exists between the lowest savage and the highest ape. The natives of Tierra del Fuego are cited as the lowest degree of savages—the gorilla as the highest ape. Not many years ago a ship touched at Tierra del Fuego, and took on board three Fuegians, who, at first savage and uncouth, became after a few weeks quite tame and tractable. Does any one suppose that the gorillas would have become tame and civilized? No. M. de Chaillu mentions that he attempted to domesticate a young gorilla, but it was perfectly untameable—it bit and flew at every one that approached, and died from the effects of its passion. These may be taken as instances of the relative behaviour of the rational man and irrational brute. Monkeys may not always be so fierce and untameable; still they never make the smallest approach to reason or civilization.

The other argument to which I alluded was one used by the Archbishop of York in his sermon at the Bradford meeting of the British Association. The nearer an ape may approach in physical conformation to a man, the more strong is the evidence that rationality in man does not proceed from physical organization, or any material source; for then the monkeys and apes would approach more nearly to man in intelligence than dogs and elephants, which they do not. No: reason is entirely distinct from the instinct of brutes—it is a gift of GOD con-
solely on man, and on no other animal.

The Evolution theory in its most extreme phase, that is, the notion that all creation was evolved out of a single seed or monad, reminds one irresistibly of "Jack and the Bean-stalk." Jack sowed a bean which sprang up and grew so rapidly that when he climbed up one fine day he found a whole brood of giants with all sorts of appurtenances evolved out of it. So the extreme Evolutionists imagine that the animal and vegetable organisms which we see around us have been evolved from a single germ.

Truly this sort of evolution might be called the "Bean-stalk Theory."

NOTE B. (P. 110.)

GERMAN METAPHYSICS.

One would have thought that the position, "Cogito, ergo sum, (I think, therefore I am,) could not be disputed, but it appears that the modern sceptics of Germany are not willing to admit even so much as that. But it may be doubted, as Dean Mansel says, whether German philosophy can be made intelligible to an Englishman. "The very authority to which an Englishman appeals in support of his instinctive beliefs, [i.e., Common Sense,] is regarded by his transcendental kins-man as an impostor and simpleton."

"The first law of all thought, the primary condition without which all subsequent reason falls to the ground, is the assumption that everything is itself, A=A"—I am I—or "the ego posits itself."

"The distribution of the universe in which German philoso-phy especially rejoices is the Ego and Non Ego, das Ich und das Nicht Ich—that is, myself and everything else."

But how can I know that I exist, that this is the ego at all? "Cogito, ergo sum," (I think, therefore I am,) says Descartes. No, answers Fichte, that is no proof; you can only say, "Cogito, ergo videor esse," (I think therefore I seem to be).

Besides, when you say, I think, it implies a thinking being; what I want is the ego without the cogito. Cogito is the self manifested in consciousness; but what is the self without consciousness? In so much as I am conscious, I have a mere phenomenal existence; what is required is the absolute, unconditioned, I by myself I. In truth the real self is an unknown and unknowable something.

Such is a specimen of modern German philosophy. Those who should happen to wish to know more about it, may be referred to Dean Mansel's lecture on "Modern German Philosophy" in his recently published "Letters, Lectures and Reviews." I will give another instance. "The consciousness of self is manifested only as accompanying any successful representation. At each moment of consciousness I can repeat but I, I, I, and always I: and thus at each moment I vanish to be produced again. . . . . There is nothing enduring, neither without me nor within me; only an unceasing change. I know of no existence, not even my own. There *is* no existence. I myself know nothing, and am nothing. Images alone are present in consciousness. . . . . I myself am one of those images; or rather I am not even this. All reality is changed into a wondrous dream, without a life to dream of, and without a mind to dream, a dream composed of a dream of itself. Perception is a dream; thought is a dream of that dream." (Fichte's Werke, ii., p. 244, 245, quoted from Mansel.)

Again: "Pure being has no distinguishing marks; in other words it is identical with pure Nothing. And thus by placing the principle of existence in the abstraction of all definiteness, we arrive at the first axiom of Hegel's philosophy—the identity of existence and non-existence." (Mansel, p. 208.)

Yet once again. Spinoza's description of GOD "extended, yet incorporeal; thinking, yet without understanding; free and active, yet without will." (P. 349.)

NOTE C. (P. 164.)

THE NATURE OF GOD.

One chief endeavour of non-Christian Philosophers, whether physicists or psychologists, is, if possible, to do away with the belief in a Personal GOD as revealed to us in the Bible. Hence the strange and uncouth dogmas which have been put forth. Mr. Matthew Arnold says that "GOD is simply the stream of tendency by which all things fulfil the law of their being," or "the enduring power, not ourselves, which maketh for righteousness." Schelling calls GOD "the Absolute Ego;" others pronounce Him to be "the Unknown and Unknowable," "the Absolute and Unconditioned," "the Force, or Law, or Order of Nature," "the Anima Mundi," "All things," anything in short but the GOD of Christians, who believe, as we have been taught in childhood, and as the experience of mature years confirms to us that GOD is our FATHER, Which is in heaven, our Redeemer, our Sanctifier, Maker of all things, Judge of all men, and that our simple duty towards Him is to believe in Him, and love Him, and worship Him, and to serve Him truly all the days of our life.

Surely the child who knows his duty to GOD is greater and wiser than many a nineteenth century philosopher.

J. MASTERS & SON, Printers, Albion Buildings, Bartholomew Close.

CPSIA information can be obtained at www.ICGtesting.com
Printed in the USA
BVOW05s1415010216

435027BV00020B/137/P